C000299614

For Ann,

Characters

I Hope You Enjoyed Reading This Book.

Albert Irving

Albert Spring, the author.

Characters

A. E. Spring

The Pentland Press
Edinburgh – Cambridge – Durham – USA

© A. E. Spring, 1997

First published in 1997 by
The Pentland Press Ltd
1 Hutton Close
South Church
Bishop Auckland
Durham

All rights reserved
Unauthorised duplication
contravenes existing laws

ISBN 1-85821-527-7

Typeset by Carnegie Publishing, 18 Maynard St, Preston
Printed and bound by Bookcraft Ltd, Bath.

Acknowledgement

My gratitude to all the families of the people about whom I have written, who have given me their blessing and supplied me with photographs and very often information too.

Contents

Characters

Foreword
by my brother John Spring

When my brother Albert told me that he was writing a book about some of the characters he grew up with or met with at various times in his life I suggested that I write a few words about him.

We were born in one of a row of eight cottages at Winwick Hill, a mile from the village of Winwick in Huntingdonshire. It was a very isolated spot and the cottages were very humble indeed with no facilities at all. Money and work were very scarce at all times and our mother and stepfather often had a job to pay the rent which at the time was one shilling a week. Each cottage had an acre of land for a garden and so it supplied us with most of the fruit and vegetables we needed. We kept our own chickens for egg laying but they often went on strike and refused to lay.

By the time Albert was about seven years old and I was a couple of years his junior he was a foot taller than me and as tough as nails.

The natural way of country life seemed to be bred into him and he hated to be indoors. He became a dab hand at making and using a catapult. My skill with it was in no way to be compared with his; he could and did kill rabbits and often hit a bird in flight. Besides the catapult he made and the snares that he set for rabbits he seemed to know by instinct exactly where to set a snare so the poor rabbits did not seem to have a fair chance. I suppose it was inevitable that by the time he was about twelve he was a very good poacher, but

My brother John Spring

of course by his skill in the fields we were all enjoying our share of the spoils: mainly rabbit but once in a while a hare or even a pheasant or partridge, the latter being killed with a catapult.

I have skipped by one item which I feel I must mention. He was never very keen on school. He was much happier out in the fields so most mornings our mother got him on the road to school with the help of a stout stick. Once he was on his way past the farm at the bottom of the hill Tom Leigh would come out with his horse whip which he would crack a few times to encourage my brother on his way.

Once in school he settled down to make the best of what he clearly looked upon as a very poor bargain but he was keen on sport, football and cricket. He also became a formidable boxer or possibly I ought to say fighter because his attitude at all times was to fight like a rat in the corner. By the time he was seven he had a dog of his own and throughout his life he became very well known for his knowledge and ability to train and work all types of dogs including terriers, lurchers, spaniels and labradors. A lot of people ask him to train dogs for them.

Once when he had more dogs in training than he could really handle he asked a very special friend if he would help him out and train a couple for him. His friend looked stunned and said, 'I couldn't do that, I haven't got a clue.' Albert said, 'Of course you can; all you have to do is teach them to sit and fetch and carry and just obey orders. 'Oh,' his friend said, 'I can do that; I thought that you expected me to train them to ride a bike or push a wheelbarrow or something daft like that.'

I will now move back to the outbreak of the last war in 1939. We both went into the forces about the same time, Albert into the Army and I into the Royal Air Force. We did not see each other after that until 1944. It was after the battle of Arnhem. I had just come home and was told that Albert, who was then a paratrooper with the 10th Battalion, had been dropped there. He along with a few members of his Battalion had been lucky enough to survive and were now back in England.

I learnt that they were in a camp just outside the town of Grantham. It was only thirty-odd miles away so I paid them a visit. They were in a large Nissen type of barrack hut and in Albert's corner hanging up behind a blanket were numerous rabbits, pheasants, and bundles of snares. On the top of the black coke-fired stove was a dixie full of rabbit stew. I only had to close my eyes and I was back in the humble cottage at Winwick Hill. I thought, good God, he will never change. Talking to his comrades I gathered that my brother was held in very high esteem because with the help of the wartime Dutch Resistance he had been mainly responsible for their escape from the enemy-occupied Holland, but one of his fellow men told me, 'It's terrible being back; I never know when I am going to get into one of his bloody snares.'

By the end of the war he was still alive. After being demobbed he got employed as a gamekeeper and was always thought of very highly by his employers and all who went in the shooting fields with him.

He is now seventy-seven and says that he is retired but I don't really believe it, it is just a myth. Now that his book *Characters* is published I hope you enjoy it, but, knowing my brother, I doubt if you have ever known a person with more character than he has.

Characters

I was born in the year of 1916 and for the first twelve years of my life I lived with my mother, my stepfather, my sister, a younger brother and five stepbrothers. We all lived in two cottages: numbers 5 and 6 in a row of eight situated on the roadside between the villages of Winwick and Hamerton in the county of Huntingdonshire.

Joe White

In cottage number 4 lived a man named Joe White. There was Joe and his wife, a son Arthur and a daughter Ethel. Joe White was a very good living person as were all his family. He often preached at Winwick Chapel.

He made a living mainly by skinning sheep and lambs that died on the surrounding farms. He would cure all the skins using mainly the salt-petre and arsenic method.

He used the cured hide which was then fine leather to manufacture hedging mittens, knee pads, and soft leather gloves. These last were made out of the lamb skins. The local farmers bought these for their farm labourers to wear when they were handling sheaves of corn. The hedging mittens were for the workmen when they were laying and binding thorn hedges; the knee pads were used by men when they were doing jobs like thatching that would mean putting a lot of their weight on their knees while they were on a ladder.

Joe also cut leather boot-laces for workmen's boots; one pair of boot-laces usually lasted as long as the boots. Joe would if asked cure a sheepskin leaving the fleece on. These made lovely rugs.

When one of my Uncle John's sheep dogs died Joe skinned it and cured the skin and my Aunt Liz and Uncle John had it on their bedroom floor for many years.

I spent a lot of time with Joe White every year when he was sowing his garden seeds. He would stand and look at his garden, stroke his long white beard and say, 'Ah, once again I sow but only the good Lord knows if I will live to reap.' He lived to be ninety-six years of age. I cannot remember all the prices he charged but one dozen pairs of soft leather gloves would cost ten shillings; if they were bought in lots of less than a dozen it was one shilling per pair.

Once when Joe was preaching at the Chapel Harvest Festival at Winwick Chapel all of us children got a very severe lecture when we laughed at Joe's preaching. We all laughed when Joe said we must thank the Lord for all the vegetables and the fruit; we must even thank the Lord for all the little potatoes and the little apples because they are all little before they are big.

Arthur White

Joe White's son was named Arthur and I used to watch Arthur very carefully because he was often using a muzzle loading shotgun and he usually let me tag along with him. One Saturday I saw Arthur go into the little barn with the muzzle loader. He always loaded the gun in the barn, so of course I joined him and said, 'What are we going after today, Arthur?' He was thirteen years older than me so it was a privilege to address him as Arthur.

After he had loaded the gun he said, 'Follow me,' and away we went along the yard and around the end of the cottages to where the Whites' chicken pen and run was situated. When we got to the pen, Arthur said, 'Mother wants a chicken for tomorrow's dinner.'

He then knelt down on one knee and thrust the gun muzzle through the chicken wire some seventeen or eighteen inches above the ground. He said, 'The first one to come and look up the barrel gets it.' Of course, after a little while one did just that and Arthur squeezed the trigger. Oh, I thought, what a perfect way to select a chicken.

It was the month of March, a dry windy day and it was Saturday. Once again I observed Arthur entering the little barn with the muzzle loader so I joined him and asked, 'What are we going to do?' He replied, 'You will see in a few minutes.'

I will explain what is done to load a muzzle loader. First of all a measure of powder is tipped into the muzzle of the gun while the butt is resting on the floor. This is followed by in this case a few pieces of paper which are pushed down tight with a ramrod. Then comes a measure of shot, then more paper again pushed down firmly with the ramrod. When this is all done the hammer is pulled back to the cocked position and the last thing is to place the small copper firing cap over the end of the hollow tube that is situated over the hole just above where the powder charge is. When the trigger is squeezed the hammer hits the copper cap which fires a flash that goes down the hole and ignites the powder which then explodes and the shot accompanied by the burning paper is discharged out of the muzzle.

Now back to the Saturday morning in March. Arthur had loaded the muzzle loader and we proceeded round to the front of the houses and stood behind the garden hedge that was along the whole of the front of the eight cottages. The hedge was about four feet in height. In cottage number 2 lived a man named John Jolly. He lived alone and was some sixty years of age. He worked on the land for any farmer who wanted work done for a fixed sum of money. For example, for a hedge trimmed and all the debris cleaned up and burned, at that time in the early 1920s, the price would be about nine pence per chain. A chain was twenty-two yards in length and pennies were two hundred and forty in the pound. John Jolly did hedge trimming, hedge laying, ditching, and land draining.

Now just over John's front garden hedge he had constructed a hovel in which he stored all the tools of his trade, spades, forks, hedge hooks, scythes, rakes, and so on. The hovel was constructed entirely of straw plaited onto a wooden frame. This was Arthur's objective. He had been throwing bread crumbs on to the roof of John's hovel to feed the sparrows and the roof of the hovel was a mass of hungry sparrows. When we were some fifteen yards from the hovel up came the gun very slowly and bang, it went spraying shot, smoke and pieces of burning paper all over John's hovel. The shot killed a lot of sparrows but it was a dry windy day and before we could get to the hovel it was on fire. We grabbed a few of the tools to try and save them but in twenty seconds it was an inferno. Then John came on the scene and you believe me, he was one angry man. He would have killed us if he could have got hold of us but we bolted away into the fields and we did not dare to come home until it was dark.

We avoided John Jolly for a long, long time.

During the next week every family came up with some sort of tool for John so that he could carry on working. They all knew that no work meant no food or tobacco. Arthur White emigrated to Australia when I was seven years of age. It was a shame really; we were very much alike. Without any doubt we would have had a lot of fun together.

George Hull

It was 1924 when the Hull family came to live at Winwick. They consisted of George Hull, George's wife (I never knew her first name), a son Fred, a daughter Nin, and a son of Nin's named Percy, but always known as Tommy. He was one year younger than me.

Characters

We were friends right up to his death in 1977, some fifty-three years on.

I intend to write about George Hull first of all. George and his wife had a number of other children who visited them once in a while. There was another grandson who lived with them; his name was George but he was always known as Ruddy. He was younger than Tommy. George was, I would think, about fifty years of age when he came to Winwick. He was a threshing engine driver by trade, about six feet tall and weighing some twelve stone.

He drank beer, he smoked twist tobacco, he chewed twist tobacco. He had a number of guns: a muzzle loader, a double-barrelled pin fire and a couple of double-barrelled hammer guns.

George was a strong man and very, very hardy; whatever the weather was doing he would do whatever he intended to do. It could snow, rain, hail, or blow: if George intended to go out after pigeon, rabbit, or any of the game birds he went. When his clothes got wet through on him they got dry the same way on him. He never removed any of his clothes to dry them. I have been in his house when he has come in soaked to his skin. He would sit down in front of a log fire in the open hearth fireplace and in a few minutes it was a job to see across the room because of the steam and tobacco smoke.

I know that in theory he should have been at the very least crippled with rheumatism but he never was. He was active all his long life. At ninety-three years of age, between the villages of Thurning and Clopton in Northamptonshire, he fell off his cycle and broke one of his thighs. He died a few weeks later and at the time he had his gun with him, his object being to shoot a few pigeons. Now I will tell you a few of his stories.

When the chimney from the open hearth fire became sooted up George had his own method of sweeping it. He would put a cartridge in the twelve-bore, poke the barrel up the chimney and squeeze the trigger. I never saw a chimney swept so quickly and effectively in all my life, the soot came down by the bucketful.

5

Characters

When George was in charge of the threshing tackle engine and, as often happened, there were numerous rats that had made their home in the cornstack, we boys would whenever possible attend with a stout stick to kill them. George however would not go to that bother. If he saw a rat running along the side of the stack he would grab it up in his bare hand and squeeze it to death. He was often bitten by the rat when doing this but he never took the least notice of that. When questiond about this he would tell the questioner, 'When the rat dies its poison dies with it, I would only be afraid if I was bitten by a rat and it escaped.'

Some of George's stories I think are hardly the whole truth.

Before moving to Winwick George and his family resided at Tilley Hill which is situated between Oundle and Glapthorn, at that time just a few cottages, now all built up area. George used to carry his gun and shoot rabbits, pigeon and so on on the land that his employer farmed. In one field a very large hare always sat in its form. According to George, his boss and a number of other persons had taken a shot at, in his words, the grut old hare but the old hare always rose from her form before anyone could get close enough for a really effective shot. 'So,' George said, 'I noticed that she went through the hedge at the same spot every time she left the field so one day I goes into the next field and sets a strong snare at the place where she always went through, then I goes back into the field that she was always in and up she gets and straight into the snare. I had caught her so I kills her and takes her home. When I weighs her she weighed twelve pound. We intended to eat her but she had so much shot stuck in her skin that it was impossible to get a knife through it.'

George never claimed to have killed a great number of pigeon with a single shot but this is his tale in his own words.

'I was pigeon shooting some distance from Glapthorn on Baker's Farm and a grut flock [he meant great flock] of pigeon came and settled in front of where I was in the hedge. There was thousands of them and I brings the old gun up and gives them a barrel while they was on the ground and the other barrel as they gets up. There was dead pigeon everywhere and some was still falling out of the flock as they flew away. I followed the flock for over a mile and then came back and picked the rest up and when I got them all picked up and counted there was just two hundred and sixty-eight.

I heard George tell that tale on several occasions, it never varied.

George was a strong man so read this one told as George told it in my presence on several occasions.

'We were threshing at a farm close to Benefield and it came on to rain and after a little while the driving belt came off so we went into the big barn and had our beer ration and just sat and talked. The talk got around to weight carrying. In the barn was a heap of sand, about a cartload. There were enough weights to weigh twenty stone so twenty stone was put into each of two separate sacks then one of the sacks was emptied into the other sack, making a total of forty stone in the one sack [this was five hundred weight]. The sack was placed on the sack winder and wound up and I got it across my shoulders and carried it around the barn for several minutes. That was no trouble at all but when I got home my old man gave me a belting because the weight had burst my boot welts out.'

When George was around seventy years of age I saw him put his neckerchief (it was like a scarf) through the handles of three fifty-six pound weights, grasp the knot in his mouth and walk along with the total of one hundred and sixty-eight pounds suspended from his mouth.

George's grandson, Tommy

Tommy and I were without a doubt a well matched pair both as lads and as adults. We both had the same interests, these being the ways of the wild. Going to school we did not enjoy but we had to tolerate it mainly for the sake of our parents.

When I was fourteen Tommy was thirteen years of age and we

were very low in the recognized standards of civilized education, but we knew more about the birds and the animals that lived in the trees and hedgerows than our educated teachers of arithmetic, scripture, history and geography were capable of absorbing.

I do not know if education is of any great advantage or not but looking at our world in the 1990s it has certainly enabled the people in it to become more adept in killing and causing all sorts of evil and mayhem in the world. The motor car immediately comes to mind. It is a very close run contest between motor vehicles and the atomic bomb as to which is the most efficient destroyer of life.

Back to Tommy. He and I by the time we left school were very good at catching rabbits of which there were thousands in our area. To give the reader some idea of what we were capable of: it was 1931 and it was February, there had been a lot of rain and all or nearly all of the rabbit burrows adjacent to the brook known as stream Hemmer were full of water which meant that the rabbits that usually resided in the burrows were above ground taking refuge on any available patch of dry land. Stream Hemmer starts at Hemington, flowing from the north-west to the south-east passing through Luddington, just missing Great Gidding, Little Gidding and Steeple Gidding, passing through Hammerton, Alconbury Weston and Alconbury, and then flowing on to join the River Ouse at Huntingdon.

Back to the Meadows adjacent to Hemmer in the parish of Winwick. It was Saturday afternoon. We knew all the habits of the local farmers and what time they went to have a look at their stock that consisted of bullocks and sheep. We knew that the safest line of approach was to follow a hedgerow that divided two farms then, if we saw someone on our side of the hedge, we, in Tommy's words, just nipped through the fence.

All we were armed with were catapults and pockets full of pebbles as ammunition. Each pebble was roughly the size of a present day two pence piece. In a couple of hours we had killed exactly forty full grown rabbits. Then we had to carry them home.

A piece of string threaded through the hind legs and slung over the shoulder bandolier fashion is the easiest method of carrying that kind of load.

The next thing was to wait until the light started to fade so that it would be almost dark by the time we reached the village and almost everyone would be indoors having their tea by the light of their paraffin fuelled lamps.

You must understand that if caught most of the farmers would have prosecuted us and any of them who did not prosecute us would have seized the rabbits. If we had been prosecuted the summons would have been headed: Trespass in Pursuit of Conies. We knew all about it, having already been to the Magistrates Court several times. It usually meant a fine of ten shillings, today fifty pence, and of course a very severe lecture on our evil ways.

Tommy Hull was in my opinion a very honest person. He despised thieves but the pursuit of conies, i.e., rabbits, hares or game, was in his opinion honest sport and preferable to doing too much work.

When we were both at school we used to catch a lot of sparrows using a round cinder sieve. You may wonder what a cinder sieve is. It is a fine wire mesh fastened to a wooden frame and usually about thirty inches in diameter. When a man or his wife cleaned the fire grate out in the morning the ashes and cinders were put in a bucket and then they would be put in the sieve. When this was shaken on the garden the fine ashes would pass through the wire mesh and the cinders were put back in the bucket to be returned to the fire.

Tommy and I would fasten a cinder sieve onto a piece of wood some five or six feet in length and then visit the corn and haystacks which were the favourite roosting places of sparrows. By rubbing the sieve up and down the sparrows would try to fly and be caught in the sieve. We never attempted to catch too many in one evening, but always endeavoured to catch just enough for our own needs.

This is what we did with them. At one end of the house in which the Hulls lived was a single storied building. Its walls were of mainly plaster commonly referred to as mud and stud; it had a rusty zinc roof and an open hearth fireplace. Usually we would collect our firewood around the fields in the hours of daylight and light the fire after we had caught the sparrows. Then we would pluck the sparrows and roast them over the fire on a piece of wire. We never removed their legs, head, or intestines. Tommy and I and one or two of our closest friends including Nin his mother became expert at eating the two breasts of a sparrow but I remember we persuaded my cousin Ernie George to join us for a meal one evening and he bit too hard when he had the wrong end in his mouth and the sparrow's intestines popped out in his mouth. We thought for a moment or two that he might actually be sick though he wasn't but he did say that little incident spoilt his appetite.

Ernie George's mother was my Aunt Kate but all the family disapproved of what they termed our wild ways although they did not say no to a free rabbit when it was offered. It is impossible to please some folk. The reader may wonder why we never got food poisoning. In that day and age I never heard of any person ever getting that complaint.

I must do a little more explaining before proceeding with the next little story or incident in the parish of Winwick. None of the land was looked after by a gamekeeper so it was only a matter of keeping an eye open for the farmers and their family and their workmen. The local policeman resided at Old Weston, some two and a half miles distant. Tommy usually referred to him as the sheriff. The whole of Hamerton Parish was known as the Hamerton Estate and was looked after by a full time gamekeeper.

The two parishes of Little Gidding and Steeple Gidding were owned during the 1920s and early 30s by Whattoff and Co. They employed a full time gamekeeper. His name was Mr Noble but we never got to know him well enough to know his first name.

Just one field over the stream Hemmer in Little Gidding parish was a small wood known as Little Gidding Fox Covert. It was some ten or eleven acres in size and there were a great number of rabbits living in that wood. We had watched them many times. Tommy said, 'Why don't we snare some of those rabbits. Noble can't be all that interested in them because if he was there would not be so many up there.'

So one afternoon we lay down and watched the wood. There were rabbits at play on the two sides that we could observe. Wood pigeons flew to and fro so we made a quiet approach and got out of sight inside the wood, being very careful in avoiding the cattle grazing in the fields. We found an easy walk path just inside the wood and proceeded to set our snares, all the time on the right hand side of the path. We did this so that we could pick them up more easily in the early morning. We had set about a dozen snares when a rabbit squeaked behind us so I walked back and two rabbits had got in the snares we had just set. I killed them and reset the snares and rejoined Tommy. We had set about another half a dozen snares and again a rabbit squeaked loud and clear so once again I retraced my steps and this time there were three rabbits so now I had five rabbits on a piece of cord over my shoulder. I walked quietly back to rejoin Tommy and found him on one knee with his right hand raised. I knew the sign: it meant extreme caution. I crept up until I was right by his side. He whispered in my ear, 'We are not alone.'

We just crouched there on the path and sure enough we could hear someone or something come down the walk path. Being down at almost ground level we could see about twenty or twenty-five yards and the first thing we saw was his legs coming towards us. There was not any convenient cover to crawl under to hide so we had to run or be caught. We chose to run, angling to the outside of the wood. We dived under the two strands of barbed wire, closely pursued by this big man who we knew as Mr Noble. We refused his invitation to stop, of course. We gained a few yards while he negotiated the barbed wire. He was accompanied by a large black Labrador dog which he repeatedly ordered to get us. The dog did not obey his order but it did run alongside us for a little way. We were running downhill on grass; Tommy was fourteen, I was fifteen and Mr Noble was fifty plus. For a start he held his own. He was trying just to catch us but we were running as though our very lives depended on it. We came to a gap beside stream Hemmer, again under the wire. The bank on that side was a foot lower than the bank on the other side. The stream was some ten feet wide and five feet deep at that point. Mr Noble was fifty yards behind. He shouted out something like, 'Ah, I've got you.'

I threw the five rabbits over the water, still on their piece of string. Two strides and I jumped up to my waist in water but with my arms and chest on the bank. I was clear; Mr Noble was fifteen yards away. Tommy was smaller than me. I was lying down on my stomach with my arms stretched out over the water. I just caught one hand and he was up on the bank with me though he had lost his cap. Mr Noble was shouting after us as we moved away, 'I know who you are; I'll have the police after you.' We did not answer him as we did not wish to annoy him.

It was about dark when we got home. We still had the five rabbits but we had lost the snares, exactly nineteen. The price of snares was eight shillings and sixpence per gross (one hundred and forty-four).

I said to Tommy, 'When did you first hear him?'

Tommy said, 'I didn't hear him; I just got that feeling, you know what it is, I just knew we were not alone.'

I did know; I was like that myself.

We were not visited by the police so we came to the conclusion that Mr Noble had not filed a complaint against us. In my lifetime I was to have a lot to do with gamekeepers and I found out that taking the average they were fairly good chaps. One other thing we found out was that all rabbits caught by Mr Noble had to be handed into the hands of Whattoff and Co. This would explain why there were always a lot of rabbits on their land.

At about this time Tommy purchased a ferret. He bought it from a gypsy who regularly travelled around our area. The gypsy's name was Rodney Brinkly. Rodney was a real character; he will be mentioned later. The ferret that Tommy had given Rodney half a crown for was a small light brown (female) jill. It did look a lot like a stoat. Tommy said, 'It's a bit fierce, mate,' and showed me the bite marks on his hands to prove it. The word fierce was one of the understatements of all time. That ferret was so bloodthirsty that it was almost impossible to handle it at all. Oh! It would go down rabbit holes after rabbit but when it was actually biting a rabbit it would let go of the rabbit and bite whoever took hold of the rabbit. There was nothing else for it so it was put in a box and sent to the local market. It was sold for two shillings. It cost three pence carriage and three pence auctioneer's fee, so Tommy was a shilling out of pocket on that deal and I bet that whoever bought it did not try taking it out of the box before they had paid for it.

The years went by. Tommy and I were to be firm friends for the whole of his life. In 1939 the war came. Tommy was conscripted into one regiment of the Infantry and I into another so the war parted us but we communicated by post once in a while. Tommy was a poor correspondent; he had not spent enough time at school to be a keen writer. We both survived and returned to Winwick in due course. Tommy was never very informative about the war. He still had his quiet dry sense of humour and a lot of scars on his body from enemy shrapnel. He once told me with a wild twinkle in his eye that he was on the Salerno Landings in Italy. This is what he said: 'We had advanced several miles and all the big guns and little guns were making a terrible lot of noise and then we were told to dig in so we dug in and then the noise got worse and in a little while we noticed that a lot of our side were going past us in the direction we had come from and they seemed to be in a terrible hurry. Then someone shouted, "You want to bloody well get out of there and come with us."' He said, 'Boy, they didn't have to ask me twice. I was out of that hole so fast that I travelled five yards before my feet touched the ground again.'

After the war there had to be a slowing down in both Tommy's and my own way of life. Both of us had married in 1939 but things had gone wrong with Tommy's marriage while he was away at the war and he and his wife had divorced.

Tommy married again and went to live at Oundle. His second wife looked after him very well and was a very kind person. He had a regular job with the Forestry Commission. Unfortunately he was taken ill and died in 1975. One of his last remarks to me before his death was, 'Boy, do you remember when Noble thought he had us trapped at the brook?' and his dark eyes glittered once again as they always did when he was excited.

It was my intention to make that the final piece about Tommy but I must tell you this. Always when he had his holiday he would spend every day with me and one day we were on my trap round. Oh yes, I took to being a gamekeeper like a duck takes to water. We came to a tunnel in which there had been a trap set and the trap had been drawn into the tunnel the full length of the chain. Without thinking I grasped the chain and commenced to pull the chain out of the tunnel and bingo, there was a very much alive male hob stoat in the trap, and of course he had a very good grip on my thumb and did not show any intention of letting go. Tommy looked at the situation in a very professional manner and he said, 'Ah, it's not unlike that bloody ferret that I bought off old Rodney forty year ago,' and as an afterthought he added, 'and I thought you had more bloody sense than to let a bloody stoat bite you.' Of course I squeezed its rib cage with my free hand and it was quickly dead.

Secretly, Tommy never changed his ways. He always looked on a poached pheasant, hare or rabbit as honestly earned but he was one hundred per cent trustworthy. A gamekeeper friend of mine was keeper on land between Oundle and Benefield. He had a married daughter living in Canada and for a number of years he and his wife would go to Canada for several weeks in the summer. While they were away he would leave Tommy in complete charge. This is what he said to me: 'When I leave Tommy in charge I know everything is OK. Tommy is one hundred per cent trustworthy, the most honest rogue I have ever known.' What a tribute.

I look upon myself as extremely fortunate to have known Tommy when we were so young and more fortunate to have called him friend for so many years.

When my wife and I attended Tommy's funeral in Oundle Church we were absolutely astounded at the great number of people who also attended at the service. Tommy was without a doubt far better known than even I realized and I was one of his best friends. A catapult should have been put in his coffin with him.

Harry Mills the gamekeeper, and my stepfather

Harry Mills was employed as gamekeeper by a gentleman farmer named James Moss Howson who owned and resided at the farm that to this day is still known as Howsons Lodge and which is situated in the parish of Old Weston. It was a model farm and was always spick and span. Every gate was painted white each year and all the hinges and latches were black. All hedges were kept neat and tidy.

Mr J. M. Howson kept three couple of beagles with which we often hunted the hares on his land. When he invited the Fitzwilliam Foxhounds to meet at the lodge, the entertainment was very lavish so it was a very popular meet. Harry Mills was his gamekeeper and lived in a cottage situated some little distance from the lodge beside the road that led to Clopton. He was a very boastful character who kept bees. I well remember a swarm of bees settling on the roadside hedge on the outskirts of Winwick and someone informed Harry of their presence. Harry said, 'I will come and collect them in the evening.' He duly arrived on his cycle with his skep. He did not wear any protective clothing, not even a jacket. He got off his cycle and approached the bees with his skep in his hand. The swarm was some four feet high on the hedge and they started to buzz. They stung Harry from top to toe but to give Harry full credit he did not flee and he eventually got most of the bees into his skep and cycled home with them. For a long time he said that swarm of bees were the nastiest that he had ever met up with. What he did not know was that just before he arrived on the scene we boys had been using the swarm as a target for our catapults; we knew why they were nasty.

Harry spent a lot of time in public houses drinking beer. This was also a habit of my stepfather, Ernest Farrer. One Sunday Harry and my stepfather had been drinking together in the Three Horseshoes situated in Winwick Village. They had been in the pub from midday to about two thirty in the afternoon and when my stepfather arrived home he ate his dinner and went for a walk. I accompanied him; we walked down some fields situated just behind where we lived. The fields were named 'Well Grounds'. Now the sporting on these

The Fitzwilliam Foxhounds meet at Hamerton. 1986.

fields was rented by Mr J. M. Howson and while we were walking who should approach us but Harry Mills, of course. It was the beer talking and Harry's talk was most belligerent. He accused my stepfather of poaching; one cross word let to another and my stepfather was a man with a very violent temper. Harry had taken his jacket off to fight. We were some fifteen paces from a large muddy pond and my stepfather promptly grabbed Harry and threw him into it. He threw his jacket in after him and when Harry climbed out of the pond, still spluttering, my stepfather just for good measure threw him back in. Of course it meant my stepfather appearing before the Magistrates at Huntingdon charged with assault. He was fined six pounds, and ten shillings costs. The next Sunday when the pub opened at twelve o'clock Harry and Ernest were drinking together again.

My stepfather was a veteran from the First World War. He had been wounded while serving in the Northants Yeomanry and received a forty per cent disability pension. This was eight shillings and sixpence per week. He was often suspected and accused of poaching but he never poached in any way at all. I knew him from 1921 until his death in 1953. He had lived all his life in Raunds in Northamptonshire up to the outbreak of the 1914–18 war and Raunds was famous for its poachers during that time.

James Moss Howson died in 1928. Howsons Lodge and all the land was sold and Harry Mills moved away.

Malcolm Groom, and the logic of a child

Malcolm Groom was my nephew. He was born in May 1930 and was brought up by my mother. We all lived in a house in Winwick village. There was a married lady in the village who was, shall we say, very well built. We will call her Mrs B as the lady is still alive. Now Mrs B walked past my mother's house several times each day on her way to see her in-laws who were old and rather infirm. When Malcolm was some four or five years of age he was standing in the open doorway when once again Mrs B passed by and this is what he said to my mother:

'Granny?'

My mother answered, 'Yes my beauty, what is it?'

Malcolm asked, 'Why does Mrs B always take her pigeons with her when she goes to her in-laws?'

My mother replied, saying, 'My beauty, Mrs B does not have any pigeons.'

Malcolm replied, 'Ah, Granny, but she does. I know because when she walks along I can see them fluttering about under the front of her dress.'

About the same time there was a funeral which took place in the village and from my mother's house the church and churchyard were in full view. Malcolm was watching all the while. There are two entrances to Winwick churchyard; one has a wooden gate and the other an iron gate. The first is the direct entrance to the church, the second to what is known as the new part of the burial ground.

Malcolm Groom.

Malcolm: 'Granny, they are carrying him in through the wooden gate; where are they taking him?'

My mother: 'They are taking him into the church.'

Malcolm: 'Why are they taking him in there?'

18

My mother: 'They are taking him in there to pray for his soul.'

Some thirty minutes later, Malcolm: 'Granny, they are bringing him out through the wooden gate and taking him in through the iron gate. What are they going to do now?'

My mother: 'Oh, they are going to bury him in the ground now.'

Malcolm: 'Is his soul in the box with him, Granny?'

My mother: 'His soul has gone to heaven.'

Malcolm, after a long pause: 'Granny, will you make me a promise?'

My mother: 'Of course I will, my beauty.'

Malcolm: 'Promise me that when I die you won't let that happen to me, because I want all my parts to go to the same place.'

On both occasions when these conversations took place I was an interested listener. I have never forgotten any of it.

Tommy Stringer

To put you in the picture, I was born in 1916. Tommy Stringer had a son old enough to serve and lose his life in the 1914–18 war.

Before my time, Tommy and his wife had resided in the village of Old Weston but sometime about the year 1920 they had moved to Winwick. They lived in a wood and plaster house that at one time had a roof of thatch, but the thatch had been replaced with a corrugated zinc roof that had been liberally coated with red oxide.

Tommy never in my time did any work on a regular system of employment. His wife, Anna Maria, kept the house supplied with food by doing washing and scrubbing floors and so on for the slightly better off householders.

Tommy would do all sorts of odd jobs to earn his beer and baccy money. He could be seen riding on his bicycle around any village in the district with a pot of tar and tar brush hanging on the handlebars. He would give the soft water butts a coat of tar for whatever the householder could afford to pay. It might be a shilling or sixpence or just threepence and if there was anyone who had fallen on hard times he would still tar their water butt and say, 'That's all right; you can pay me when times are better.'

Please understand that in the 1920s every household owned one or more soft water butts; they were always of wood. Soft water, which was rainwater, had to be caught in a wooden container. If it was caught in a metal container it was not recognised as soft. I often wondered about this because in lots of instances, the water had in the first place fallen onto a metal roof, perhaps zinc. Soft water, when available, was very much preferred for the washing of all household linen.

In the same period nearly all lavatories were either bucket or pit and Tommy specialized in the cleaning out of pit lavatories. But however Tommy earned a few shillings, it usually went on the purchase of beer. He was a very cheerful man and I never met a living person who spoke a bad word against him. He would go off on his bicycle in his corduroy trousers and cap and jacket of the same material. He would have a coloured neckerchief around his neck and leather boots, and for a great number of years a large brindle coloured lurcher trotting alongside his cycle. If he earned a shilling or two it was always well past turning out time before he arrived home. Anna Maria was short tongued and she would say, "Tussit, Tommy, wherever have you been till now?" and Tommy would chuckle and say, "You know where I have been, my gal." As far as it is known there was never a cross word said between them.

The lurcher's name was Captain. It had a reputation of being a great catcher of hares and rabbits but I do not believe this to be true. I saw Captain and Tommy together for a number of years and I never saw the dog show the least interest in the sight or scent of these creatures which abounded in the area. Nor did I ever observe Tommy carrying a suspicious bundle of any sort, nor did I ever meet a person who had seen Captain in action in pursuit of a hare or rabbit.

Tommy would be having a few pints of beer, which in the 1920s was four pence and five pence a pint, the one penny difference being if a person drank mild or bitter, and sometimes a person who didn't know Tommy very well would show an interest in Captain. After a few tentative questions, Tommy would praise his skill and cunning when after a hare or rabbit, adding as an aside, 'He is always getting me into trouble.' If the comparative stranger took the bait and asked Tommy if he would sell the dog, Tommy would empty his glass and say, 'If I had a pint I would sell the old dog,' and of course the stranger would buy him a pint, obviously thinking he had got himself a good dog for the price of a pint of beer but when he said, 'Right, I'll take the old dog now,' Tommy would say, 'Oh no, I said if I had a pint I would sell the old dog; I did not say that I would sell him for a pint.'

I knew this to happen on a number of occasions but Tommy never left his own area and when the would-be purchaser of Captain looked around and saw everyone's eyes on him he usually kept his peace. Every local person thought a lot of Tommy Stringer and if anyone even threatened Tommy he was a wise man if he made himself scarce as quickly as possible.

Tommy died just before the Second World War. His wife Anna Maria lived on into the late 1950s. She was well into her eighties and died at Thurning.

George

About this person, there is not a lot to tell. He was a yardman on Gidding Grove farm, situated about one mile from Winwick in the parish of Great Gidding. He was married and had two daughters.

A person employed as a yardman on a farm was responsible for the cattle, the rearing of calves, the pigs, in some cases the sheep as well and sometimes the poultry. Some liked to be known as the stockman, but George always preferred to be known as the

The hornets' nest in my cabin, 1981.

yardman. The time was the late 1920s and early 1930s, just before and just after the time I left school.

We had a boys' club at Winwick and George was a member as were a number of adults; the oldest boy was seventy plus.

George could tell a good tale and this is one of them. George's father was employed as horse-keeper at Denford Ash lodge, a couple miles or so on the south side of Thrapston. His employer was a Mr C. Nichols; the time was the early 1920s. George's father's name was Sam.

One morning, Mr Nichols remarked to Sam, 'Those trees behind the big barn are getting too tall; I think they are dangerous. We ought to get them lopped so I will see about getting someone to attend to it.'

Sam says, 'Yes, master, I think you are right but I don't think you need to go to the trouble of getting anyone else to do it; I think we could manage that job.'

'Right,' said the master, 'I will leave you to see to it.'

So on a quiet day Sam and another workman named Jack Hunt carried a forty round ladder and stood it up against the first tree. They then carried a thirty-two round ladder to the same spot. Now this is what George told us, he said, 'My old man climbed up to the top of the forty round ladder taking the thirty-two round ladder

22

with him. He then stood at the top of the forty round ladder and balanced the thirty-two round ladder on his knee and Jack Hunt went up the forty rounder and then up the thirty-two rounder with his saw, but,' George said, 'it was no use because he was nowhere near the topmost branches of the tree.' Note, the forty round ladder would be approximately forty feet, the thirty-two rounder approximately thirty-two feet, so whenever I hear anyone talking about tall trees I always think of George's tale about the tall trees at Denford Ash.

Just one more little tale that I heard George tell on several occasions, again about the 1920s. To my knowledge, George had two sisters and this is what he told us: 'My sister worked at the laundry, at Thrapston and at home. She had put three goose eggs under a broody hen, but after about three weeks the broody hen decided that she was no longer interested and left the nest. My sister could not find another broody hen and was at her wits end about what to do. The eggs required another week of incubation so as a last resort she put the eggs under her blouse, between her breasts, and kept them there for a week. Then one day while she was working at the laundry she had to ask the manageress if she could go home because her goslings were hatching.' George said they all hatched out all right.

Tom Roe

Known by the nickname of Tom Tit, he was a native of Winwick, one of a family of three boys and four girls born and reared in a small white-washed thatched cottage standing in its own half acre of garden and fruit trees with a pond just about fifteen yards from the one and only door. The cottage had two bedrooms and two downstairs rooms. When all the family were at home it must have been a struggle to find sleeping space. Two girls were younger than me, the other five children were older. The mother was an invalid and had to be pushed around in a wheelchair for the last thirty years of her life, but I do not ever recall seeing any member of the family with untidy or dirty clothes.

Although Tom Tit was some seven or eight years older than me we were somehow drawn together although we had rather different interests. Mine were always more the ways of the wild whereas Tom liked to go out and about. He was a very nice, clean, tidy and good looking young man, but thinking back I cannot remember him ever dating a girl or walking one home. Funny, but I never thought about that aspect before.

If it was a fine evening on a Sunday during the summer months Tom Tit and his sister Alice could be seen pushing the wheelchair with their mother in it along the road, usually to the village of Thurning, which was a distance of two miles from Winwick. They would have a drink at the public house named the Wheatsheaf and then return home. The Wheatsheaf was kept at that time by Arthur Clarkson and his very good wife; they were a very nice couple and such kind good natured people.

About 1930 Tom Tit caught a very bad chill and it developed into pneumonia. I remember visiting him. He was propped up by pillows on a single bed in the kitchen, and his sister Alice was nursing him. She had a huge iron saucepan hanging on an iron hook over the fire that burned in the open fireplace. There were two kettles steaming away on those paraffin burners that had to be ignited with methylated spirit. It was almost impossible to see across the small kitchen for steam, but at least the treatment worked because Tom Tit made a full recovery.

Some three years later when I was seventeen we all went to the October fair at Peterborough. This was a big fair held each year. There was in those days all sorts of entertainment: swings, coconut shies, dodgems, you name it, it was there. Anyhow, we were standing outside one of the boxing booths, numerous boxers of various weights were on parade and the booth manager was looking for challengers for his men from the onlookers. Tom Tit suddenly grabbed hold of my right hand and shouted, 'Here you are, here's one,' and that was it. I found myself in the boxing ring facing a professional looking opponent with whom I was expected to fight over three rounds. Fortunately I was very fit, very quick and had been used to sparring at our boys' club for a number of years and I survived the bout without any serious injury. The reward was a share of the coins that were thrown into the ring by spectators, who had already paid the handsome sum of sixpence to enter the booth. Anyhow I received ten shillings as my share and when I later said to Tom Tit, 'You are a great mate, trying to get me half killed,' he said, 'Don't you realize that was the easiest money we ever earned?' I liked the 'we' bit.

When I was over eighteen years old we used to get on our bikes every Saturday evening and go to any village where a dance was being held. There were always several to chose from and on this evening we chose to go to Molesworth some six miles distant. Of course we had to have a beer or two at the public house in that village. It was named the Cross Keys and at that time it was kept by two sisters named the Miss Throssells. The Cross Keys is still there but the Miss Throssells have passed away though they both lived to a very old age.

The evening progressed to everyone's satisfaction and it was all right until Tom Tit, who was our star entertainer on these occasions, stood up on the taproom table to perform a tap dance which he accompanied with one of his little songs. In this case it was titled, 'I want to sell my Mary'. Anyhow, one of the Miss Throssells objected to Tom Tit dancing on the table and took hold of his trouser leg, telling him to get off her table, now. Unfortunately Miss Throssell was blessed or otherwise with more than average whiskers on her face and of course Tom Tit stopped singing and very politely replied, 'Madam, I will dismount from your table if you will have a shave.' That did it. Oh! The lady was angry and quite rightly so because they were two of the nicest, kindest and most popular ladies anyone could ever wish to meet.

Only the regular customers were allowed to stay, all the non-regulars were turned out.

Fortunately, through a very good friend of ours who was a regular (he lived at Molesworth) we were given permission to visit the Cross Keys and apologise, which in due course we did and everything was as before but no more dancing on the table. The good friend's name was Jack Culpin and his wife was the girl who some years earlier, according to her brother, had hatched the goose eggs in at least a very novel way.

Yes, it's a small world.

Tom Tit was a very good entertainer. He always said, 'If I have the price of my first drink when I enter any public bar, that is enough to ensure me an evening's drinking.' He had a very fair voice and although he had left school at the age of fourteen years, he could converse in a very educated way. When going out he dressed very well indeed in white shirt, dicky bow and on special occasions a high silk hat.

His favourite songs were 'I want to sell my Mary' and 'Patrick McGinty's goat'. I cannot recall the numerous verses, but this is how the chorus went of 'I want to sell my Mary'.

I want to sell my Mary
For she's always on the booze
I want to sell my Mary
And an offer I won't refuse.
Take her and try her
Before you buy her
For that's the way to choose.
Heigh boys, clear the way
For I have a young lady for sale.

Patrick McGinty's goat went something like this:

Now Patrick McGinty
Was an Irish gentleman of note;
He came into a fortune

26

So he bought himself a goat.
After Patrick bought the goat
He named it Little Lil,
But when he went to milk her
He found Lil was a Bill.

There were somewhere around a dozen verses to these two favourite ditties, Tom Tit knew the whole lot by heart. I have never seen any of it in writing, and have no knowledge of their origin. Possibly they are something that Tom Tit made up; I never heard any other person sing them at any time.

Tom Tit often got us into trouble, but he was basically a very kind person. If he had a shilling he would share it with a friend, without being asked.

In our little group of the middle thirties who knocked around together there was Tom Tit, Harris George, known as Beamer, Jim Turner, myself and Mable George. Beamer and Mable were my cousins. Sometimes Tommy Hull would be there, also George and Bert French from Aldwinkle; we had some wonderful times.

Just before the war Tom Tit moved to Thrapston to live with his sister Alice, who had married a man named Tom King. Tom Tit got a job at Islip furnaces where they mined and extracted iron from iron stone. It was a reserved occupation. The war came and I went into the army; I was never to see Tom Tit again.

Sometime in 1944, he arrived at my mother's house at Winwick, riding a two-stroke motorcycle. He had tea and supper and stayed the night, had a good breakfast and shortly afterwards said, 'Cheerio, I am leaving now,' and rode away on his two-stroke. Later that day he was found dead by the roadside close to Hatfield, having taken his own life. My mother told me that while he was in her house he was no funnier than he always was.

I think it was a very sad end to one who had always been or appeared to be a very happy man.

Alfred Roe

Alfred Roe, always known as Alf or Stumpy, was a younger brother of Tom Tit. Alf was my senior by about one year. It would be in my opinion very unfair not to write a page or two about him.

When Alf was about seven years of age he was in a hayfield where a grass cutter pulled by two horses was at work mowing the grass. Alf chased a rabbit and jumped in front of the mower cutter bar before the horses could be stopped by the driver, Alf's left foot was neatly amputated.

Now this is what happened. He was carried to the nearest house; it happened to be a farmhouse. Then someone went and got hold of my aunt Kate who was Mrs K. George, and was a person who never got into a panic. Aunt Kate checked the flow of blood and bound up the limb very tightly with towels, then Alf was taken to the nearest doctor, who lived at Oundle, seven miles distant. He was taken there by a horse-drawn cart known as a buggy; of course the horse or pony was a fast trotter. The doctor did what he could for Alf and then got him to hospital. Alf survived.

Alf returned to school and for a long time he looked weak and thin but slowly and surely he got stronger. He had two under-the-arm crutches, made out of straight sticks with a T piece across the top. The T piece was well padded with cloth. After a year or so he was playing football and any other games that we played; he took part in everything we did including boxing.

Time went on and Alf, like the rest of us, finished with school at the ripe old age of fourteen years. He went to work as an apprentice to a Mr Cotton at Thrapston. Mr Cotton owned a boot and shoe shop and also carried out all repairs to those articles. I purchased all my boots and shoes from his shop for a great number of years.

Thrapston is ten miles from Winwick and for years Alf cycled the ten miles to Thrapston in the morning and the ten miles return journey in the evening. He did this in all weathers, having a leather strap on his cycle pedal so that his one good foot pushed the pedal down and also pulled it up again. After he had learned at least a little bit about boot and shoe repairs, Alf would carry out repair work in the evenings for the local people, to help to supplement his very meagre wage as an apprentice.

Now one may think what one likes about what I have written about Alf but this is what I think: Alf deserved all the best of everything for his determination, his tenacity and his courage. Remember, when this happened in the very early 1920s there was not any welfare state and nothing just meant nothing. Alf married a young lady who was also employed at Cotton's shop and they lived in Thrapston. Alf, I believe, worked at Cotton's for all of his working life. He was possibly not a character as much as his brother Tom Tit, but what a model for any of our generation to seek to copy.

Alf Roe died at his home at Thrapston 1 November 1992.

Steve Hunt

While I was still at school and we lived up at Winwick Hill, there was a middle-aged man who delivered the newspapers every Sunday; it was always the *News of the World*. His name was Steve Hunt and he was employed by a Mr Jellis as a horse keeper on the Grange farm at Hamerton.

Every Sunday morning Steve would cycle to Brampton, a distance of eight or nine miles, collect the papers and deliver them to the families living at the local farms and villages. He usually arrived at Winwick between midday and one o'clock, and always had a cup of tea at our house. When he collected the papers at Brampton there would be a huge canvas shoulder bag full and another large bundle on the front carrier of his cycle so he was well loaded.

Steve did this for a number of years and then, around the 1930s, Mr Jellis left the farm and Steve moved to Barham which is some two and a half miles from the Grange farm at Hamerton. Steve no

longer delivered our Sunday newspaper. The price of the newspaper was two pence, this was in today's money just four-fifths of
our one pence piece.

During the 1930s I saw Steve just once in a while, then the war
came and I was in the army for six years. I came out of the army in
1946 and in 1947 I was offered the job of gamekeeper for a
syndicate who shot over the parishes of Leighton Bromswold and
Old Weston and some land at Spaldwick. At that time it was good
partridge country.

One day I was cycling through the village of Barham and I saw
an old man working away at clipping and tidying up the roadside
hedge in front of the only farmhouse in the village. I recognised
him at once, it was Steve Hunt. I stopped and I said, 'You are Steve
Hunt, how are you getting on?'

Steve was chewing twist tobacco. He had a good look at me and
gave a little spit, then he shook his head and replied, 'No boy, I
don't remember you,' so I said, 'Steve, I was the little boy in Ern
Farrer's house on Winwick Hill when you used to deliver the *News
of the World*.'

'Ah,' he said, 'I 'member now all right,' and then he replied to
my enquiry as to how he was and this is what he said. 'Well, boy,
I am all right, but a while ago I really got messed up with them
bugging matics, I had a job to walk about, then one day I got a lift
in a motorcar down to Alconbury to see my old mate Jackie Barber.'
(Jackie Barber was I believe the last blacksmith to practise in
Alconbury.) Steve said, 'I ask Jackie how he was keeping and he
was all right; Jackie ask how I was and I told him, "Jackie, I am all
screwed up with the bugging matics; I don't know how to get
about." Jackie said, "Now, Steve boy, don't you worry; before you
go I'll give you some advice and something to put that right," and
when it was time to leave he gave me a quart bottle of harness oil
and he told me, "Now Steve, my boy, when you gits home you git
that in to you well." It took some stomachin but I got it inter me
and in a day or two the matics had all gone and they ain't been

back.' Then as a kind of afterthought he said, "And do yer know, when my girl [that was his daughter with whom he lived] tried to wash my vest, pants and shirts, they wouldn't take water cause they were so full of that oil.'

I believe that what Steve told me was the truth because I do not believe he could have fabricated such a story unless it had actually happened.

Billy Yeomans

Billy Yeomans was a native of Great Gidding and for a great number of years he resided in a house facing the Main Street in Great Gidding. Like his father before him his trade was harness making and repairing. I refer to harness that is used on horses. Billy was an excellent tradesman and, making new or repairing, he would always state the day and time by which the work would be completed. He and his wife Liz had one child, a daughter. They had a range of buildings and kept cows, using the milk to rear calves. They also kept a lot of poultry. They rented some land, I believe it was about twenty acres, some of which was down to grass for the cows to graze on and to grow enough hay for winter feed. Some was ploughed and they kept one horse to work on the land. The ploughing was usually done by the housewife Liz so as soon as Liz had got around her household duties she would harness the horse and go to plough. For a great number of years Billy worked six days a week usually down on the Fen farms in the Whittlesey area. His job was feeding a threshing drum.

Now I will give you a rough description of Billy's work programme. It was impossible for any person to work harder. I believe that he did go to bed on Saturday and Sunday nights but this is how it would go for the rest of the week. On Monday morning, he would rise before five in the morning, milk the cows and feed the calves. While he was doing that Liz would pack up his food for the day and get breakfast ready for him. By six o'clock he would be on his way to Whittlesey on his cycle. It was one hour's cycle ride and work commenced promptly at seven on the Fens. All labourers started work at seven, then they had a lunch break at eleven, usually half an hour, and then they worked on to about four o'clock in the afternoon. Then Billy would cycle back to Great Gidding. He would arrive home and get a cup of tea and some food and then commence work in his shop, making and repairing all sorts of harness and during harvest time repairing binder canvases. He worked at his bench until he fell asleep but he always awoke before five o'clock and started the same sequence all over again. He told me on a number of occasions that he usually went five days and nights without taking his boots off. The funny thing was he always appeared to be alert and bright and cheerful. No man could work harder than that no matter how he tried. As he and his wife got older he stopped going to work on the Fen and then in the early 1960s they moved around to a house at Chapel End, Great Gidding and kept the Post Office. There also Billy was getting more time for his hobby which was bell ringing. He also delivered the mail at Winwick, very often walking the whole time.

He had a very large allotment that he worked with a machine known as an iron horse. His iron horse had a seat on it so Billy could ride to and from his house and allotment when they lived at Chapel End. Bill always asked me for a dozen pheasant eggs each season; these he hatched under a broody hen and then he reared them for killing and eating when required.

When Billy was on his post round he always asked if there was any mail for posting: of course, that was when the householder was at home. Eventually Billy purchased a car, a rather ancient Ford Popular. This is what he told me one day when I asked him how he was getting on with it. He said, 'It's all right, Albert, I took Liz and our gal to Wansford last Sunday but it ain't too safe, mate, on that old A1. Do you know, we were just helling it along that road and they were passing us as though we was standing still and you know, Albert, we was doing a good thirty.'

In 1963 we had a lot of deep snow and it lay for a long time. Billy still delivered the mail and one day when he was struggling through snow two feet deep I said, 'Billy, you should have given it a miss today.' I thought he was going to faint; he replied in a shocked voice, 'Albert, whatever the weather the Royal Mail must get through.' Pony Express sentiments.

And so it went on. Billy's daughter got married and had a bungalow built on the right hand side of the Main Street and when her mother died in May 1975 the Post Office was taken over by Doreen and her husband who kept it for several years. Billy still lived at Chapel End and still worked on his garden and his allotment besides his business as harness maker although now that horses were no longer used in any numbers on the land it was a dwindling business. All the work that Billy did on horses' harness was done by hand.

By the early 1980s, Billy's health was failing. Although he was as bright and cheerful as ever he was having a lot of trouble with his feet and this eventually led to first one then the other foot being amputated. After this he was fitted with two artificial limbs. Of course they were a good bit shorter than the originals and Billy had never been very tall so he would often say, 'They [by 'they', I suppose he meant the doctors] have really cut me down to size now,' but all through these events he never grumbled or lost his sense of humour.

All the years that I knew Billy he would give you a weather forecast free of charge and it was based entirely on quarter days and moon phases and was always very close to being accurate.

A man who was scrupulously honest, of great character and faithful to his friends, he died on 12 August 1985 having lost his wife Liz in May 1975. Billy was eighty-five years of age.

Peter James Wilfred Turner, Jim

This is not easy for me. It was 1931 when I first made the acquaintance of Jim. I was fifteen years of age and he was twenty-three. I knew him by sight as I had seen him in the football field. He played for Old Weston; he was a native of that village. Old Weston is some two and a half miles south of Winwick.

In 1931 I was employed on Mount Pleasant Farm and a man came to cut and press up a clover stack that the farmer had sold. The hay presser's name was Rockley and his helper was Jim Turner. On the second day I visited that stack for the purpose of clearing up any clover that had been discarded by Rockley. Please understand that any damp or discoloured clover would be cast on one side; the buyer would only pay for the best that was in the stack. It would be carted to Barnwell Station to travel by train and it would be

Left to Right: Jim Turner, myself and Malcolm Houghton moving pheasant poults 1981.

weighed on the weighbridge by George Ashby who was the station master.

Jim and I got talking to each other. He was a very wiry type of person standing five feet eight or nine and weighing some eleven stone or thereabouts, quite good looking with eyes that seemed to glitter. When he talked we found out that we had a lot of common interests so a friendship started that was to last for the next sixty years.

I saw Jim every day at some time during the time that Rockley and he were pressing the clover into bales of approximately one hundredweight each. We talked mainly about the night nettings to catch rabbits. Jim had several long nets and claimed to be a first class man at that job. Of course most night netting was carried out by poachers and although I knew of a few persons who had lost their nets when keepers or farmers had caught them red-handed the

35

persons concerned had always got away mainly because night netting was always carried out during the hours of darkness.

Perhaps I had better explain some of the basic facts about the art of night netting for rabbits. First of all the net. This is usually knitted by hand and the mesh is usually four inches square in size, the height four feet and the length from fifty to one hundrd yards plus. At the time that I am writing about all nets were made of hemp, nylon thread being unknown at that time. A net would be put on its cords, one cord at the bottom and one at the top; if the cords were fifty yards in length then the net would need to be some seventy-five yards in length so that when it was pegged up it had plenty of loose mesh for the rabbits to become entangled in. The net was hung on a wood or iron peg in loops of about one and a half yards each loop. The person dropping the net would walk backwards, letting the net off the peg loop by loop. The next person followed him with a quiver of hazel pegs some half to three quarters of an inch thick and some three feet in length, sharpened at one end. He would give the bottom cord of the net a single twist around the pointed end of the peg then he would press the pointed end of the peg firmly into the ground and give the top cord a double twist around the top of the peg and then if everything was correct there would be seventy yards of net on fifty yards of cord held up by some six or seven pegs at a height of about thirty inches, hopefully exactly between the rabbits that were out in the open field filling their bellies and the cover they would run for when disturbed. At fifteen years of age I was very well versed in the ways of the wild, having spent more hours in the fields and woods than I had spent in the classroom or indoors with my family.

I had been out night netting since I was seven with my stepfather and his brother in law, Walter Downing, who was a gamekeeper of course. It was, I believe, carried out legally but knowing what I know now, legal or not they were not very successful night netters.

It was early spring when I first met Jim and we had become firm friends as the year went on, so by September we had planned a night netting for rabbits. We asked George Farrer who was my step-brother to join us. George was all for it.

So towards the end of September Jim came to Winwick bringing a one hundred yard long net with him in a sack and we set off for our first big night at long netting for rabbits. We had even discussed the problem of the best method of carrying home the vast numbers that we expected to catch.

Like politicians, we were to find out by experience that very often everything does not turn out according to the original plan. We were netting fields that had a hedge all round them, naturally choosing the hedge that we thought the bulk of the rabbits would run to when disturbed so in the dark we ran out the net and got it pegged up about midway off a hedgerow some four hundred yards in length. I had observed some fifty or so rabbits sitting out in the afternoon sunshine that very day. Jimmy stayed at the net: whoever stays at the net waits at one end with his fingers holding the top line very lightly. When a rabbit gets in the net he will feel the vibration quite distinctly. He then walks quickly along the front of the net until he locates the rabbit, grasps the rabbit by the body in one hand and feels for its head with the other. Once he has found the head he puts his thumb behind the head at the base of its skull with the fingers under the jaw and just levers the head back. The neck is broken and once a person gets the technique it is a very quick and simple operation. The rabbit is left in the net until the whole of the operation is over. Rabbits very seldom squeal in a net at night when they struggle in darkness.

George and I had gone right around the field, one on one side and one on the other exactly like two sheep dogs in 'One Man and His Dog'. The lift could not have been very good because when we had worked our way right back to the net we had caught a grand total of two but, forever true optimists, we carried on to another field. The same procedure was carried out only this time I stayed at the net and we caught three rabbits. But I had distinctly heard an old buck rabbit give the alarm signal and he was very close to the net. I had observed this on numerous occasions; one could lie and watch any number of rabbits sitting and nibbling grass outside their burrows and then at the alarm note of a bird – it might be a jay, a blackbird or a chaffinch – an old buck rabbit would give one stomp with both his hind feet on the ground and every rabbit in that field would sit up fully alert. If there were no more stomps, in a minute or so they would return to their nibbling but if that old buck gave two stomps in quick succession, the whole lot just disappeared before a person could blink an eye.

When I had been out with my stepfather and Walter Downing we had often used three hundred yards of netting at one set but we had never caught the great numbers that I had often heard the old timers talk about who practised that art of night netting.

I have strayed from our first night netting for rabbits so I come back to that night. We had been out one and a half hours and it was now midnight but we carried on. Then it happened. Jim was walking backwards paying out the net while I was pegging it up. Suddenly I heard Jim swearing and grunting on the ground. He had put his foot in a rabbit hole and dislocated his knee. Under his instruction I put my foot in his crutch and twisted his leg until it clicked back into place. He said this often happened. It had been caused in the first place by playing football. Anyhow we called it a night. We had been out poaching for three hours and we had caught five rabbits which were worth sixpence each: the grand total of half a crown. On our way home as he limped along Jim was already telling us of how and where we would go netting when we went again. He also said, 'I will get a new elastic bandage for my knee.'

Oh yes, we went again many times though it took a long time before we got it right, but get it right we did in 1952. Jim and I ran out and pegged two hundred and fifty yards of netting and caught fifty-two rabbits in one set. We had a mile to carry them so we went home but we went out on the following night and caught exactly fifty-two again in one set. When we were carrying the rabbits home on each night we had twenty-six each on cords slung bandolier fashion and as we walked along I kept hoping that Jim would say let's stop and rest for a minute but he never did. Once loaded up he would never stop for a rest; he was as tough as steel.

Before I write more about Jim I will give any would-be night netters for rabbits a few words of advice. First of all the nets. White nets at night are nearly useless as rabbits see them and do not run into them so use tan or green coloured nets and do not have any one net more than seventy-five yards in length. If longer it gets very heavy for one hand when picking up. Most important of all, only operate when the weather is right: that is a dark dry night and a good breeze. Of course since the advent of myxomatosis in 1953 there are very few areas where rabbits are numerous enough to be worth the effort.

Throughout the whole of his life Jim's indomitable spirit showed

Left to Right: R. Thompson, Y. Dawkes, Jim Turner, T. Masters. Talking it over, 1991.

in everything he did. Of course he was one of the party at Molesworth when Miss Throssell turned us all out through Tom Tit's
ungentlemanly remarks.

In the middle 1930s Jim and I had a couple of winters rabbit
catching at Barnwell which is now owned by the Duke of Glouces-
ter. At that time it was owned by a Major Colin Cooper who was a
big man in the International Stores. His headkeeper was Mr Algar,
a very knowledgeable man. He employed us and paid us four
shillings per dozen for the rabbits we caught. Unfortunately Major
Colin Cooper died from meningitis and everything was sold. All
the while we were rabbit catching at Barnwell Jim never grumbled.
We would set off each morning on our cycles to ride the five miles
to Barnwell. Jim would have a box of ferrets on his back and a bag
containing purse nets. I would have a sack on my back containing
a lurcher bitch named Spider; she was quite content to be carried
in a sack with just her head out. Spider used to catch us a lot of
rabbits.

Whatever the weather, Jim never grumbled. I am sure he would
have carried on rabbit catching all night if I had not have said,
'Right, we have done enough for today.'

Jim got married in 1938. The war situation was looking more
serious every day. Of course it eventually did happen and first
myself and then a little later Jim became just two more numbers in
the Army.

We both survived, I suppose more by luck than skill on our part,
and after the war we as nearly as possible picked up where we had
left off. In 1939 Jim lived at Great Gidding and I lived at Winwick.
Again it was rabbits and rabbit catching right up to the winter of
1953; that was when that horrendous disease myxomatosis nearly
eliminated the rabbit population in our countryside. It was to be a
number of years before the rabbits built up partial immunity and
even to this day, some thirty-nine years later, rabbits die from the
disease.

At the time when myxomatosis happened along I was employed

Sorting the game in Groves Wood, 1978.

as a gamekeeper and Jim as a labourer on contract work on the wartime airfields in our area so we were all right but we just did not get as much fun out of life although rabbits did build up in a few years to quite reasonable numbers. During the years of the great scarcity Jim and I still did many things together but our greatest interest in life was to observe the slow return of the rabbit. Of course it did not suit a lot of the farming fraternity. One person who farmed locally called to ask me if I could help him out because there were too many rabbits on his ground but he got off on the wrong foot when he said, 'I wish myxomatosis had killed the bloody lot.' He looked shocked when I replied, 'Yes and I wish it had done the same to the bloody farmers.' I did not help him out; that was in 1991.

Jim worked full time until he was seventy years of age and when he retired in 1978 he accompanied me every day. I was still fully employed as a gamekeeper as I was not sixty-five until May 1981.

He did the trap round at the time of the year when I was busy with the rearing. He was a good trapper. After 1981 we carried on for the same people for another ten years on a part-time basis which meant full time work for part time pay but we were happy. We were able to go rabbit catching with ferrets and fox catching with my terriers. I must tell you about a few of the amusing things that happened from time to time.

One day we were out after foxes. We visited a drain that went from one ditch to another, a distance of some three hundred yards. All we had with us were two terriers and a bag of fox nets. The drain was obviously used so I put a net on one end and Jim entered a terrier at the other. The terrier began to bay but there was no movement and the baying was within thirty yards or so of my end. Of course we knew that there must be more than one fox in the drain. After a little while I signalled to Jim to come up to my end which he did. I said, 'You watch the net while I go up to the van and get some tools.' The van was about half a mile away so I was away for some fifteen to twenty minutes. When I got back to Jim he was cleaning blood off his hands. A fox had bolted into the net and Jim had been a bit careless when he grabbed hold of it and had been bitten but he was quite happy because he had managed to master the fox with his bare hands. He said, 'I thought for a few minutes I would have to bite it.' Some ten minutes later a second fox was in the net.

On another day we were after rabbits with the ferrets and a ginger coloured rabbit bolted into a net. Jim was watching. Jim would never deliberately kill a coloured rabbit; he always said it was unlucky to do so. 'Anyhow,' he said, 'I am letting it go,' and he just shook it out of the net. Of course it promptly dived straight back down the hole it had come out of and of course the ferrets were still in the burrow. The rabbit refused to bolt a second time and the ferrets refused to leave it so it meant half an hour's hard digging to recover the ferrets and the ginger rabbit. Jim still insisted on giving the rabbit its freedom.

Please understand that those little incidents took place when Jim was in his eighty-first and eighty-second years as did the last incident I will now tell you about. For a number of years Jim's hands were so stiff from the rheumatics that he could no longer break a rabbit's neck while it was still in the net so he used to remove it from the net and then dislocate its neck by the stretch method. One day he was removing a rabbit from a net and when he had done so he just dropped the live rabbit on the ground and went to pull the neck out of the net. Oh, he did swear at me because I laughed!

I can assure all and sundry that to be out with Jim was a privilege. One never knew what he would come up with next.

We lost him for ever on 21 May 1991.

Rodney Brinkley

Rodney Brinkley was a travelling man. I believe his correct name was Rodney Harris. He and his wife and two daughters travelled the country with their caravan, horse drawn of course. Rodney also had two brothers, Arthur who always travelled alone and Reuben who had a family. I knew both Arthur and Reuben but not very well for the simple reason that they did not visit this area as often as Rodney and his family did, but they all had one thing in common. They always had a lurcher dog along with them, usually several of them. Lurchers are part greyhound running dogs; the gypsies like Rodney always called them 'long dawgs'. Rodney and his family were regular visitors in our area both before the Second World War and after. They never caused any trouble. Rodney's wife would hawk clothes pegs and lace around the villages. Rodney sat beside the fire outside their caravan and made the clothes pegs but of course they all did seasonal work when it was available. They always made their way down into Kent for the cherry picking season, also hop picking and other fruit, then they would get back onto the Fens to work in the sugar beet fields in the late spring. Everywhere they went they had their long dawgs. These were very well educated and if a gamekeeper or policeman was observed they would on command disappear into the caravan. Of all the travellers that I knew in the days of the horse-drawn caravans very few could be called serious poachers. I know that Rodney and his clan only took rabbits and hares that they required for their own daily use. Whatever they killed they skinned, cooked and ate on the same day. I know all this because I often as a young man sat by Rodney's camp fire and accepted his hospitality.

One evening Rodney said, 'I know I can trust you, boy, and I want you to do a little job for me,' and he brought out a single barrel bantam fourteen pistol, the type sometimes favoured by poachers and at that time available over the counter at any gunsmith's. All a person required to purchase and own one was the money to pay for it and a ten shilling gun licence. Anyhow, Rodney asked me to give it a good clean and oil it for him which of course I did. Ten years later and after the war Rodney would still bring his little gun for me to clean and oil and at that time I was a full-time gamekeeper. Rodney would just say as he said before, 'I know I can trust you, boy.'

I once bought a year-old black lurcher dog from Rodney, paying him five pounds for it. This dog was never a good rabbit catcher; he just never got the knack. A year later Rodney called to see me and he said, 'How did that black dawg turn out?' and when I told him he was not a good rabbit catcher he was very surprised. When I said I would like to give him back to him as a present he said, 'I'll take him back but only on the condition that you have your money back.' I had to accept the money to get rid of the dog. Rodney was the person from whom Tommy Hull purchased the biting ferret in 1931.

Bob Knight and a few others

In the middle 1930s all the locals would meet on Thurning Feast Sunday and so there would be a good gathering at the Wheat Sheaf pub. The landlord and landlady were Arthur Clarkson and his wife and a jolly couple they were. Of course it was a rather small pub with a thatched roof. There was a tap room and a best room but the price of beer was the same in both rooms. There was not a bar and all refreshment was fetched from the cellar. Thurning Feast is actually on 25 July each year so we always claimed our own feast on the Sunday nearest that day and believe me it would always be a wonderful gathering of country characters. One of these was Bob Knight, a native of Hemington. To give you a rough idea of his age at that time, he had a grandson of roughly my age.

On the Sunday I am writing about Bob came to Thurning Feast in a motor car driven by his grandson Tom. It was a Singer Eight. Now prior to this Bob had always arrived at Thurning Feast on a little two-stroke motor cycle. My memory may be at fault but I believe it was a Royal Enfield; they always flew a little green pennant on a little steel pin fixed on the front mudguard with 'Royal Enfield' emblazoned on it. Of course they were the days when the British were so proud of what they manufactured.

Bob entered the Wheat Sheaf and sat down without speaking a word. Arthur brought him a pint of beer in and put it on the table. Bob had not ordered but Arthur knew the requirements of all his customers. Bob then pulled out his pipe and tobacco and proceeded to fill his pipe. Once filled he then lit his pipe with a match. None of these old pipe smokers would ever use a petrol lighter to light a pipe. After a couple of puffs Bob picked up his pint and took a tidy drink. Then he looked around the room at the old acquaintances that were present. They all acknowledged his gaze and as though it had been rehearsed one by one they asked about his health.

After questions and answers were settled to everyone's satisfaction someone said, 'Bob, I see you arrived in style by car.'

45

Bob smiled; he liked to smile, I think mainly because he had a number of gold teeth. 'Yes,' he said, 'Tom brought me,' and of course the inevitable question: what about your motor bike? Bob took another puff at his pipe and another drink and said, 'I have packed it up.'

The room went dead quiet until someone found the courage to say, 'Bob, whatever made you do that?'

Another puff and another drink.

'Well,' Bob said, 'I was overtaken.'

'But,' said the person who had found the courage to ask the first question, 'there is no shame in being overtaken.'

Bob took another puff and another drink. 'Ah,' he replied, 'some weeks ago I was proceeding at my usual tearaway pace along the street of Stilton and I was overtaken, yes overtaken, by a young lady pushing a perambulator, so I thought it was time to give up my motor cycling activities.'

Always at Thurning Feast there would be Tom Roe with his little songs 'I want to sell my Mary' and 'Paddy McGinty's goat'; also there would be Elmer Kisby with his favourite song. I can remember the chorus but not all the verses. It went like this:

> What is the life of a man
> Any more than the leaves
> A man has his seasons
> So why should he grieve
> Although in this fine world
> He appeareth fine and gay
> Like the leaves he will wither
> And soon fade away.

There was Ernie Leech. Ernie always looked young; he was no more than five or six years older than me. His favourite was 'Willy's last Woodbine'. It went something like this.

Five little Woodbines

Characters

In a dainty little packet
Five little perfect tubes of joy . . .

My memory plays me up – I wish it was a lot better – but I know it finished up '. . . and the policeman took Willy's last Woodbine away'.

Of course the local policeman who lived at Barnwell some two miles distant never missed Thurning Feast. I can remember his name quite well. He would be there; he loved a pint and I never ever heard any person say a word against him.

I must put this little bit in. The landlord at the time was a friend of mine and he was the last landlord of the Wheat Sheaf before it was sold and became a private dwelling.

This was how it went. A real good gathering in the Wheat Sheaf, it was around midnight and up turns the local policeman in his police car. He walks in. 'Now then, landlord, don't you think it is time you turned these people out?' he asks. The landlord replies, 'Bloody hell, mate, be sensible; the pub was empty until you had turned them out everywhere else.' This is absolutely true. I have deliberately omitted the names of all persons concerned.

A word about the Singer Eight in 1932. A then great friend of mine, Bill Mayes, was a partner in a garage known as North Park Garage at Kettering. Bill Mayes sold a second-hand Singer Eight to Sid Knight of Thurning for the princely sum of three pounds. He gave Sid a write off vehicle of the same make and year for spares. Sid Knight worked at Corby. He was still using the same car to go to and from his work when war was declared in 1939. If you do not believe me ask Sid Knight; he is still alive and lives at Thrapston.

How times and cars have changed.

It would be wrong if I left what I have written about a few of the characters at Thurning Feast without mentioning Jack Norwood. Jack was the last village blacksmith to practise at Thurning. He also owned and drove a motor vehicle that by today's standards could only be described as a minibus. For a great number of years Jack transported the school children from Thurning to and from Clopton school five days each week and when Thurning cricket team played away they always travelled in Jack's bus. Jack always remarked that the bus always travelled home all right because the beer suited it.

Jack could usually be found in the Wheat Sheaf in the evening. He drank Guinness when he could get it and he loved a game of cards. He was a great snarer of rabbits, and one of his hobbies was collecting silver threepenny pieces.

Then there was Dick Short. Dick was a strong man and a great character once he knew you as a reliable character. He had a gun and always a lurcher type of dog, also a ferret and he could set a good snare. No one should ever have been surprised to see Dick pop up at any time of the day or night at any spot in the parish of Thurning.

He had one peculiarity: he did not have a single hair on the whole of his body. He told me that as a lad he had had plenty of hair but when he was thirteen years old he was walking alongside a horse that was pulling an empty cart in the harvest field on a farm that to this day is known as Kitty Grey's and there was a gallon jug of beer hung on the horse's hames. Dick said the horse tossed its head and the jug fell off and hit him on the side of the head. He said it didn't hurt him but inside of six months he had lost every hair he ever had. He always said, 'I reckon it was horse mange.' Anyhow, no one ever saw Dick take his cap off, only his family in their own house.

A little explanation about the beer jug. When I was a boy and a young man they were very common. The jug was an earthenware bottle with a corked top of usually one gallon capacity. The bottle was contained in a wickerwork frame made to fit and always had a little handle in the shape of a ring. The old timers would put their thumb through the ring and balance the bottle or jug on the top of their wrist and forearm to take a drink. I bet they would be collector's pieces now. Hames were made of wood and metal and fitted onto a work-horse's collar at the top.

The two ends stuck up like a pair of horns, again very collectable today.

In the late 1950s Dick sent word for me to go over and see him. He was old and unwell. He said, 'Albie, will you do me a favour?'

I replied, 'Dick, you know I will.'

He said, 'I want you to put my poor old dog down and bury her for me.'

Of course I did as he wished and there was a tear in his eye when I refused his offer of payment. I bet he was remembering all the rabbits and hares his old dog had caught for him when they were both a bit younger.

Fred Leech

Fred Leech was the father of Ernie Leech and Ernie was older than

The other end of the trap when set to catch.

me. Fred always looked to me such a kind and distinguished man but when he had had a beer or two he would sometimes give us a splendid rendering of that old favourite, 'It's only a beautiful picture in a beautiful golden frame'. Fred had a nice voice. That is all I shall write of Thurning Feast and its characters.

Walter Chapman

Walter Chapman was wheelwright, carpenter and undertaker at Leighton Bromswold. His son Ralph is several years older than I am. In the late 1940s and early 1950s the whole of the parish of Leighton Bromswold was part of my beat as a gamekeeper; it was partridge country.

Walter always addressed me as Ted. How this came about was that Walter and my father had played for the same cricket team before the First World War. My father's name was Edward Spring so I was Ted. In 1953 my stepfather Ernest Farrer died and Walter undertook all the funeral arrangements of course. His workshop was by the roadside in the village of Leighton Bromswold; it had double doors facing the road or perhaps we should call it the street. About four days after my stepfather's death I was cycling along the street and I saw that the workshop doors were open and Walter was in the workshop so I stopped and enquired about his health. Walter replied, 'OK, I am OK, Ted boy.' He had his coarse working apron on and his pince-nez type spectacles perched on the end of his nose. He had a piece of wax in one hand and a cloth in his other hand. He had been putting the last polishing touches to my stepfather's coffin. The coffin was made of fine grained oak.

Walter stopped working and looked at me over the top of his spectacles and he said, 'It is just about finished, Ted boy, what do you think of it? Here,' he said, 'you run your hand over it,' which I did. 'There,' Walter said, 'It's beautiful, you know it is,' and then in a soft voice as though it was an afterthought he added, 'It is beautiful, Ted boy, you know that would last anybody all their lifetime.'

I reckon that was real pride in his workmanship; please understand that this was all spoken in a very serious manner.

I still have the receipted account for digging the grave, vicar's fee, making and supplying oak coffin, solid brass fittings, shroud etc., four bearers, filling in grave and tidying up. Each item had its separate charge against it. Total £29 7s. 6d.

We have come a long way in the last thirty-nine years; it is now 1992.

Johnty Bright

His proper name was John Bright but as far as I can recollect it was always Johnty. He was one of a family of ten boys and one girl. Many a time Johnty told me of the time when they were all young. The house they lived in was thatched; it had two small rooms downstairs and a ladder led up to a trap door above which was a room that a normal sized person could not stand upright in. There was a small window at the gable end and the room was littered down with clean straw. A large, coarse linen sheet was laid on the straw and that was where the ten boys slept. Their mother and father and sister slept downstairs. I remember the house very well; it stood on the east side of the Old Weston road exactly opposite the old bakehouse until they were both demolished in the mid 1930s.

All the Brights were ordinary hard working people, honest and trustworthy. Johnty never married; neither did his brother Charles known as Wag. These two lived in a small brick built cottage opposite the Three Horseshoes at Winwick. When I was still going to school they must have been in their late fifties and were both employed on different farms, but for a good number of years Johnty had been employed as a groom by Mr J. M. Howson at Howson's Lodge.

Johnty was a member of our boys' club. He rented a large allotment about five hundred yards from where he lived and when I was about twelve years old he asked me to help him on it, so I did. I helped him dig it, plant it and then gather the crop. His allotment was a hundred yards long and about eight yards wide. At the end of the year Johnty said, 'Right, now I will treat you. I will buy you either a new bike or a new gun.'

Of course I did not hesitate: it was a new gun, so on the next Saturday we cycled to Oundle and he bought me a new double barrelled folding shotgun, four ten calibre. It cost £2 10s. 0d. I then had to get a licence. This was no trouble; a person young or old could walk into any main Post Office, pay ten shillings and receive a licence. To own and use a shotgun your name would also go up on a list that was displayed in the Post Office for all to see so of course my brother and stepfather soon found out about the licence but I kept the gun at Johnty's mainly because I had no intention of letting my stepbrothers get hold of it. We were far more civilised in those days.

Johnty and I had a lot of sport with that gun. Johnty would lean on the gate and watch for the farmer or the policeman while I went around the hedgerows and shot rabbits. There was only one trouble: even a four ten going off makes a big enough bang to be heard a mile away.

What I have written about Johnty makes him out to be a real extraordinary character so I will tell you what was his favourite story. When Johnty was young he had a friend named Frederick Burton. We will call him Fred. Apparently Fred was a bit of a lad and one day he said to Johnty, 'You come with me, mate,' so Johnty went with him. They went down the lane past the churchyard into a paddock known as Mathew Afford's paddock. Whilst walking, Fred confided to Johnty that he could fly. He was carrying two flagon baskets under his arm. Flagon baskets were constructed entirely of straw and varied in size from twelve inches by twenty inches up to almost double that size. All farm workers used flagon baskets to carry the daily food in.

Once in the paddock Fred proceeded to climb a tall tree and when he reached the upper branches he put the flagon baskets one on each of his arms and then he shouted down to Johnty, 'Now, mate, after I have gone don't tell anyone about it because if you do they will say you are not sharp.' Johnty said, 'And then he flapped his arms and he jumped and didn't he come a purler; it sure knocked the wind out of him. It took him a long time to get his wind back.'

Toll Sharp

Only on two occasions in the whole of my life was I privileged to meet Toll Sharp. When I was thirty Toll was over eighty years of age. At the time Toll resided at Fenstanton, some sixteen miles east of Winwick. In his heyday Toll had been a legend as far as it was possible to be in the field of owning and working terriers that went to ground to fox and badger.

In 1948 or 1949 I went with Tubby Lupton and a number of other persons to remove badgers that had made a nuisance of themselves by establishing themselves right beside a telephone exchange on the south side of the A604 Huntingdon to Cambridge Road. The exchange was almost opposite the road to Hemingford Grey. We had only just got out of our vehicles when a car arrived driven by a young man. There was an elderly gentleman with him: it was Toll Sharp of whom I had heard so much. Tubby introduced me to him. Toll was a man of medium build with very bright blue eyes. He wore thick all leather knee breeches, brown boots and brown leather leggings from ankle to knee. Terriers were entered and we were successful in taking the badgers alive. I did not get much opportunity to talk to Toll.

Several weeks later we were in that area again, this time at Somersham and Toll was with us again. He and I got talking about hunting and foxes and terriers and so on. And this is the story that he told to me. It was before the First World War and a gentleman had invited the local foxhounds to meet at his large and palatial house. There was a large gravelled area in the front of his house in the centre of which was a planting of ornamental trees and shrubs. The planting was some twenty yards in length, about twelve yards wide at the broad end and narrowed down to a point at the other end.

'One week before the meet was to take place the gentleman sent for me,' said Toll, and when Toll arrived this is what the gentleman told him. 'Now you know I have asked the hounds to meet here in a week's time. I want you to get a good live fox for me and before the meet you will hide in that shrubbery and you will have the fox in a bag. Then when they are all taking their stirrup cup you will tip the fox out and when the fox bolts out of the shrubbery we will see if they can ride with a glass of sherry in one hand.' Toll said, 'All through the week I tried to get a fox with my terriers. I found several but I lost the lot, usually by it bolting out of a hole that I had neglected to net or had not seen.'

Toll told me that he had no opportunity to inform the gentleman of his dismal failure so the meet of hounds took place as arranged. Toll said, 'I kept out of the way, but as everyone accepted the gentleman's lavish hospitality a fox leapt out of the shrubbery in full view of the hounds and horse people and fled for his life.' Toll said, 'Albert, that gentleman refused to believe that it was not a bagged fox.' I believe Toll; truth is often stranger than fiction.

Biff McKale

Of course it would have been an impossibility not to have met up with a number of characters during my time in the Army, especially during the 1939–45 conflict and of all the characters that stand out there was one character that I will always remember. He was an

Irishman. I did not ever get to know him all that well but I will tell you about him. I found myself a member of the Eleventh Scottish Commando in July 1940 and we were at Galashiels in Scotland. The unit consisted of ten troops with fifty-three officers and men in each troop making a total with the administration personnel known as headquarters of almost six hundred persons all told. Perhaps I should have said 'gentlemen' because the first time our colonel addressed us his first word was, 'Gentlemen.'

One week later we were on the Isle of Arran in civilian billets and commencing intensive training. As training progressed we began to get to know each other; when the time could be found inter-troop boxing matches took place. Of course we were all young men including our officers. Now one man stood out above the rest in the middleweight division; his name was McKale, known as Biff. He knew all the dirty tricks and most of the clean ones. Biff was from the Irish Guards. He had been a boy soldier and became a guardsman when he was eighteen. He was six feet tall with a face that looked as though it had been carved out of rock, a body that looked as if it was made of whip leather and steel sinews. Always clean, with knife-like creases in his uniform, when he joined the commando in July 1940 his rank was guardsman which is equivalent to private in an ordinary Infantry unit. After six weeks in the commando he was a sergeant.

Slowly the history of Biff leaked out. He had on several occasions while in the Guards risen in the ranks up to the rank of Regimental Sergeant Major but he had one big weakness which was not entirely unknown among his countrymen. Booze was his first weakness and his second was that when he got booze he had that terrible habit of becoming very quarrelsome and so it always ended up with a brawl. Usually this meant that Biff would be up on orders for brawling and so all the time that I knew him he was up and down in rank like a yoyo but up or down, he was always a very very smart soldier. Neither did he lack courage. When we were in the Western Desert Biff always had a crease in his uniform and was always clean and shaven. In fact I looked on him as a model soldier. I have no idea what happened to him as our paths separated towards the end of 1942 but I am sure of one thing: that was, give Biff booze at the right time and place and the Afrika Korps would have been kaput. Three cheers for Biff McKale!

4985070 Private J. Beet

From January 1943 to September 1944, Joe Beet was a member of my platoon in a company, the Tenth Parachute Battalion. This Battalion had been newly formed and had undergone its parachute training in Egypt on the banks of the Suez Canal. In the last few months of 1942 Joe, like the majority of us, was a conscript. We kidded ourselves that we were civilians masquerading as soldiers. Joe's home town was Derby. He was a tremendously popular person with all persons he came into contact with but he had an absolute horror of jumping out of an aircraft. He would tell us fellow paratroopers who were behind him in the aircraft, 'Keep pushing me until I am out of that bloody door.' It is true, we could smell his fear although Joe told us his fear was not the only thing we could smell, but he always got out when he was in the aircraft. The sweat would run off his helmet strap like a tap and his lips would be going as if he was praying. When asked if he was praying his reply was, 'Hell no, I am cursing my bloody mates who incited me to volunteer in the first place.'

Once he was on the ground he was all right. He was number one on a Bren gun and always absolutely reliable. We were up in Tunisia just outside Sousse in May 1943. The North African campaign was over and the German Afrika Korps had been defeated. Our Company Commander was a career soldier. He was an excellent commander and as soon as hostilities ceased in Africa the order came out that we were to tighten up on discipline and generally smarten up. Of course our kit bags had caught up with us and our mail as well. Then when my platoon officer was inspecting the platoon one morning we instructed a number of the men to get their hair cut. Joe was one of them and so the next morning, parading in battle order, the platoon was once again inspected. When the platoon officer and I got almost abreast of Joe, Joe took a step forward and removed his helmet. He had had his haircut all right and his comrades had shaved his head until it was as bald as a pound of lard. Of course this caused a lot of amusement in the platoon.

On the evening of 9 September 1943 our battalion on board the Royal Navy battle cruiser *Penelope* sailed, or perhaps I should have said cruised, into the harbour of Taranto in Southern Italy. At 2000 hours we were leaping onto the quay and we were on Italian soil, or concrete. The Italians had signed a treaty with the Allies to the effect that their war against us ceased at midnight on 8 September. We met no opposition at all although the Royal Navy mine-laying cruiser, the *Abdiel*, was blown in two by a moored mine in the harbour. All this happened as we advanced at the double to secure the town. Of course Joe was there as large as life. His hair had grown by this time. We force-marched north-east in the direction of the Port of Bari which was, at a guess, over a hundred kilometres away. Two days later we came up against the first serious opposition from the enemy. They were German paratroops. We advanced onto a small town named Castellanetta and got into the outskirts of the town. The most serious loss was the death by machine gun fire of our divisional commander General Hopkinson.

Castellanetta was built on an escarpment and all along the main road the houses were on the right and on the left of the road there was a wall some three feet in height. Outside the wall the ground fell away very steeply. We advanced along the road, weapons at the ready. Joe was in No 1 section and was on the left of the road by the wall. It was evening and the light was just commencing to fade when we came under machine gun fire, one directly from the front and one from a side street on our right. Of course we quickly brought fire to bear onto the enemy positions. We could not see the enemy but they were using a lot of tracer ammunition so the situation was soon under control. We pressed on for about another quarter of a mile then a message reached us to the effect that we were to take up a defensive position for the night. A casualty report was requested and a report on our ammunition.

Then we made an alarming discovery. Joe and his Bren gun were missing so we began a search. L/Cpl Jack Storey said that he thought Joe had jumped over the wall when we were first fired on so we went and looked. That is what he had done and there he was fifteen feet below the top of the wall, not daring to move. He was up to his neck in a stinking morass of rotten tomatoes, grapes left over from the wine making and a lot of other stinking debris. All that could be seen was his head and one arm. We said, 'Are you OK, Joe?' and he was, so we commenced to get enough pieces of cord to get him out. That dump was like quicksand; there must have been forty or fifty tons of it. While we were getting ready Joe shouted out, 'What are you doing, messing about, get me out!' His best mate, to comfort him, said, 'Stop worrying, Joe, we are just voting to see if we get you out now or leave you until tomorrow.' Eventually he was got out. Fortunately he had kept a grip of his Bren gun. Joe got really shirty when someone commenced to talk about that little ditty, 'Violets sweet, violets sweeter than the roses.' That little incident helped to take the tension out of the brief action.

There are to my certain knowledge still a few persons alive today who know what I have written is true but Joe rests with a number of the members of that platoon of that time. Yes, he is in that beautiful cemetery full of airborne troops at Oosterbeek in Holland. That is all I intend to write about war-time comrades. So back to Civvy Street . . .

William Lupton

The first time that I met this man I knew why his nickname was Tubby, it just had to be. He was five feet nine in height and weighed usually about twenty-four stone.

We first met in the springtime of 1948. I was a gamekeeper on a partridge beat that included the parishes of Leighton Bromswold and Old Weston. Salome Wood was part of my beat; this was a wood of some fifty-seven acres and it was all in the hunting country of the Fitzwilliam Foxhounds. In Salome Wood there were numerous badger sets in which were many badgers. The local hunt terrier man, Jerry Hankins, informed me that a number of persons were coming to Salome Wood to remove some of the badgers on a certain Sunday morning. When that day came I was there waiting and the first van arrived just before nine o'clock. In the passenger seat was this big man. He got out and walked over to me. He looked at me for about a minute as though I was a horse then said, 'So you are Albert Spring.' I said, 'Yes, that is my name.' His eyes, which were very blue, twinkled and he just said, 'I am Tubby,' and held out a huge right hand. We had met.

The younger man who was driving the van was David Johnson. In the back of the van were eight terriers, all white with black or tan markings. Several of these terriers stood sixteen or seventeen inches at the shoulder and must have weighed a pound for every inch in height. All had old scar marks on their muzzles and they certainly looked a workmanlike lot. I was soon to find out that they knew all about underground work and how to look after themselves.

At that time I owned a couple of useful terriers that would go to ground to fox although the main purpose that I used them for was hunting rabbits.

During the next few minutes a number of other persons arrived including a Mr Thomas Searle who resided at a farm named Eldernell just outside Whittlesey. He was also a magistrate. He had brought along a fair amount of beer, bread, butter, ham and cheese and other food. Then there was Lew Lyons from Ramsey and Jack Smith from off the Fen who had come along with Sam Poles. Sam practised as a vet at Whittlesey. There were also Bill Cad from Blatherwyke and Tip Mills from Holbeach. Before the war Tip had been a grass and cinder track racer on a motor cycle. There were several other persons whom I did not know but it was time to get down to the business of badger digging which we did. All of Tubby's terriers were excellent at finding badgers and we did dig and take three badgers. During that day we certainly moved some soil.

It is perhaps time to tell you why we did this. If there was a large population of badgers in any hunting country it was very difficult to hunt a fox very successfully above ground. The foxes knew every badger sett in the area and quickly went to ground so for good hunting it was best if there were not too many setts.

As time went by I and several of my friends were to accompany Tubby and what was termed Tubby's Gang on a great number of badger digging expeditions. I found out that any person who ever followed foxhounds, otterhounds, or any other form of hunting hound, they all knew Tubby. It mattered not where it was, Tubby was known. Tubby's profession was train driving; he was often driving express trains. How he got the time off to attend the meets of a number of packs of foxhounds and a number of days with the Bucks otterhounds or the Courtney Tracy I will never know, but he did.

Never in my life did I know anyone who could eat or drink more than Tubby and still stay upright. I will tell you about one incident. It was 1956 and we went to the residence of a Major Mountjoy Fayne. It was at Holywell some six miles east of Stamford. The headkeeper there was Charlie Payne. They had been having trouble with badgers. Oh yes, I know from first hand experience that badgers are not the good well behaved creatures that a tremendous number of persons would have us believe. They are not all rogues; neither are they all good.

Tubby Lupton, with terriers, and Lord Tom Fitzwilliam. Photographed at the Boxing Day meet of the Fitzwilliam Foxhounds 1962.

We arrived at about nine in the morning and went to a large badger sett in a wood some five hundred yards from the big house and we soon got down to business. After a while Major Fayne visited us. The Major said to Charlie Payne, 'Take a couple of these chaps down to the house; there is some refreshment for them.' Three of them went and when they returned they brought with them a case containing two dozen pint bottles of beer also two baskets containing bread, butter, ham, cheese and cake and in one of the baskets was a sealed bottle of London Dry Gin, pint size.

Tubby quickly got the work and the refreshment business organized. He just said, "Right, you and you carry on digging; the rest of you get some beer and food and then change with the ones who are working." He took the bottle of gin out of the basket, gazed at it for a moment, and said, 'It's a waste to share this, there would not be a lot for each of us, so I will have it,' and he proceeded to do just that. He sat down on the upturned beer crate and just drank it out of the bottle. It was quickly gone. Oscar Jordan from Little Staughton who was digging with me at the time remarked to me, 'He will pass out at any time,' but he did not; he just got some bread, butter, ham and cheese, ate it, drank a bottle of beer to wash it down and carried on as though it was an everyday event. It did not appear to have any noticeable effect on him at all. Never having been a great drinking person myself, the very thought of that bottle of neat gin made me feel ill.

If anyone ever reads about all this they will think that I knew some rum characters; well, they would be quite right, I did and still do.

Having become one of what was termed Tubby's Gang certainly led to a lot of different parts of the country being open to us. It also meant a lot of work and entertainment. We visited North Luffenham Golf Course regularly. At that time there was a good number of badgers in that area and the management did not like the way the badgers treated their golf course. Once a year they gave us a good meal and refreshment for our efforts.

Now about the cruelty aspect of all this. Tubby Lupton would not allow any unnecessary cruelty at any time. If a badger was to be destroyed it was destroyed quickly and humanely; also, whichever terrier found the badger to ground, that was the terrier that stayed with the badger until it was dug up. I have never seen an example of so called badger baiting so I do not really know what is meant by the term. Over a period of twenty years we only had three terriers that received enough damage from badger or badgers to require veterinary treatment.

I well remember going to Leighton Gorse with Tubby and the Gang. It was 1959 and the local fox population had been decimated by what was termed fox encephalitis. This was supposedly brought about by eating dead pigeon that had died through eating seed corn that had been treated with a seed dressing named Deildrin. In a number of places badgers had been found dead showing exactly the same symptoms as the foxes. We were accompanied by two vets from the Burroughs Wellcome Laboratories at Cambridge who had brought a couple of strong wooden boxes to transport any live badgers to Cambridge for examination in the laboratories there. The boxes were heavy so they were left in their van. The badgers would be carried to them in sacks.

Terriers were entered and we were soon digging. We dug up to the terrier which was picked up and there was a good adult badger which was picked up by the tail and the back of the head and put in a sack. There was another badger in the same hole. This was treated in the same way. One of the vets had the neck of the sack firmly in his hands and Tubby said, 'Swing it over your back, it won't bite,' so the vet swung it up and over his shoulder. As he turned away, Tubby pinched his backside hard between his finger and thumb. The vet shouted out, 'It has bloody well bit me,' and promptly dropped the sack. Of course out popped the badger and dived into another part of the sett. It was two hours hard digging before we captured it a second time.

On a number of occasions during that year we were requested to obtain live undamaged badgers for research on encephalitis, also undamaged dead badgers were required. These we killed by placing a container of ether over their muzzle and they were very quickly dead. The vets told us that encephalitis affected the brain of both fox and badger. After Deildrin was banned it did not occur again.

I remember a comparative stranger passing a remark to Tubby that most of his terriers looked like Parson Jack Russells. As quick as light, Tubby replied, 'No, they are Tubby Lupton terriers without the Parson.' It was a sight to see Tubby exercising four or five couple of his terriers along Mountsteven Avenue. He would be seated on his bicycle, all twenty-four stone of him, and the terriers would tow him along by their leads. I once remarked to him, 'What happens if they view a cat?' He smiled and this is what he said. 'I always carry a hunting horn and before I set out I give a couple of tootles on it and then as we go along the only cats we see are sitting up on the trees. Oh yes, we have them well trained, the cats, I mean.'

In July 1963 Tubby suffered a massive heart attack that killed him. It was also ironical that during the extremely cold and snowy weather in January, February and March of that year his terriers developed a coughing virus that killed practically all that he had at home. Of course he had a number lent out to various friends and hunts. Very well do I remember a number of their names: there were Jack, Sam, Joker, Leslie and Ben, all dogs; there were Lady, Sage, Sally, Sue and June, all bitches, and of course there were always the younger ones coming along. One of Tubby's favourites was Lady. He always laughed about the time he entered Lady in a working terrier show and when the judge looked in her mouth he said, 'Good God, she has not got a tooth in her mouth.' Tubby thought that was a great joke, he said, and poor Lady never got a prize.

Like Tubby each and every one of his terriers was a character.

Harry Penfold

Before the war Harry was a travelling man but when the war came all travellers had to become static. Harry became static in a field on the north side of the road from Old Weston to Clopton. The name of the field was Chaney's Copse. It was grass at that time, surrounded with a high hedge and a number of trees. Sixty yards away was a large deep pond, so water was not a problem. The field was the property of Mr Fred Chapman who lived and farmed at Titchmarsh Warren Farm about one mile from Chaney's Copse.

I made the acquaintance of Harry in January 1940 just before I went into the Army. He was a tall, slenderly built man with brown eyes. His family consisted of two boys and two girls. The youngest girl was in 1940 some five years of age and looked very pale and thin. Her mother had died soon after her birth. Her name was Tuppence. I did not meet the older girl until after the war because she was in a sanatorium for TB sufferers. Both boys were in their early teens and seemed surly until one got to know them. Harry also owned a horse that was normally used to draw his caravan.

It was December 1940 and I came home on fourteen days' leave before being sent overseas. I went to see Harry as I was always made welcome. Of course I was in my civilian clothes. I had walked up the fields and had a shotgun with me. On the way I had shot two rabbits and a hare. Of course I gave them to Harry and he thanked me in a very nice manner.

We talked over a cup of tea and Harry suddenly said, 'Albie, I thought you was in the Army.'

I replied, 'Yes, I am, but while I am home on leave I am what I was before I was called up.'

Harry seemed to have difficulty in understanding the whys and wherefores of that so on the very next afternoon I put on my full uniform including my webbing equipment with my rifle and fifty rounds of ammunition and cycled by road and visited Harry. He was over the moon. His most serious question was, 'Do you take it all off when you go to bed?' Harry was not feeble-minded, far from it, but he had never learnt to read or write.

It was January 1944 before I saw Harry again. During the time that I was away his little girl had died and this is what my mother-in-law told me. She lived at Clopton and also did the church cleaning. When Tuppence died Harry got the local undertaker to make a little coffin for her, then he sought out the vicar who administered Clopton church and obtained permission for her to be buried in the churchyard. There the only persons present when this took place were Harry and his two sons, the vicar and my mother-in-law. Harry's sons had dug the grave and eventually filled it in. Of course the church register had to be filled in and the vicar, looking at the death certificate, said to Harry, 'This just gives the child's name as Tuppence Penfold; had the child no other name?' Harry just said, "When she was born she was such a little tiny thing that her mother said to me, she is no bigger than two pennorth of coppers, so we always called her Tuppence.'

In January 1944, almost the first thing I noticed when I entered Harry's caravan was that Harry had a pair of spectacles on and that there were newspapers in the caravan. After a little time spent talking I questioned Harry about the spectacles and newspapers. This was his reply. 'I went to Peterborough on the bus and bought the spectacles at Woolworths. I had decided to learn to read and now my elder daughter comes home more often she promised to teach me.' He said, 'Albie, I hates work and so I thought that if I learned to read I would see in the papers the day the war was finished, then I need not work any more.'

My stepfather always purchased his glasses from Woolworths. The cost was sixpence a pair old money.

Just after the war Harry purchased a spinney; it was just over one acre in extent. He paid forty pounds in cash for it and he told me it cost another forty pounds in solicitor's fees etc., only Harry used a far less polite word than 'solicitors' to describe them. It was called Bishop's Spinney and it was situated just below Chaney's Copse, no more than four hundred yards from Harry's caravan. Harry and his sons gathered all the rotten and dead wood in the spinney for burning and cleared a lot of the old undergrowth and burned that up. Then Harry planted hundreds of daffodil and tulip bulbs and numerous other flowers and it was certainly a pretty place.

In 1953 my stepfather was very ill, in fact he died that year. All through his illness Harry sent or brought flowers for him. They had worked together during the war and of course often enjoyed a pint of beer together. A few years later when Harry's health broke down he sold the spinney to a local farmer who bulldozed it all level just to grow a few more tons of wheat. I salvaged some of the bulbs and they survive to this day in my front garden.

Harry had to go into a home to be looked after but he did not survive for very long. His two sons moved to Huntingdon and I have not seen either of them for many years.

What happened to his older daughter I do not know; she was a very pretty girl.

Herbert Webb

The first time that I met Herbert Webb was shortly after the last war. Herbert was a native of Raunds which is situated in Northamptonshire. He was a small man, possibly five feet six or seven in height and weighing round about eleven stones. His nickname was Captain, possibly because of his habit of walking up and down with his hands behind his back whenever he was talking, and he did a lot of talking.

For the whole of my lifetime the small town of Raunds was notorious for its poachers. They were not poachers who carried guns, no, they were men who poached after rabbits with ferrets and snares, but they were best known for their ability as knitters of long nets and of their knowledge in the use of the long nets. Persons who constructed long nets or even small bolt or purse nets by hand were known as knitters and the speed at which they knitted had to be seen to be believed. A bolt or purse is a net two feet six square and the two ends are fastened onto metal rings. A fine cord is passed through each square around the edge and through the rings. A peg is attached to the two ends and pressed into the ground. The net is placed over a rabbit hole and when a rabbit bolts into it the line is held by the peg and the rabbit is in the net exactly as if it was in a purse, hence the name bolt or purse net.

If and when I required top quality nets for fox, rabbit or rat I only had to let Herbert know and they were usually ready inside forty-eight hours.

The main industry at Raunds, except poaching, was the manufacture of boots and shoes. In between the two wars all the best quality boots and shoes for the whole of England were made in Northamptonshire.

In the middle 1920s a gang of night netters was apprehended on the Kimbolton Estate. Herbert was their lookout man and he was the only one to escape, all the others being caught by the Estate gamekeepers and the police. It meant being locked up for that night then eventually appearing at a Magistrate's Court and having to pay a fine of a pound or two in each case but of course the hardest blow was the loss of five hundred yards of nets. Herbert escaped and carried the sad news to Raunds. He said the whole of the population of Raunds went into mourning.

During the winter of 1978 Herbert and an old pal of his were ferreting rabbits at Catworth. Herbert was seventy-nine and his companion was eighty years of age. They were ferreting a sett or burrow beside a very deep dyke, almost full of water. Herbert's companion, hurrying to grab a rabbit that had got in a bolt net, slipped and went into the water in the dyke. Herbert ran to help him out but also finished up in the water. Fortunately they both got out. They then picked up their ferrets and tackle, walked to their car, drove home to Raunds, a distance of some eight miles, changed their clothes, drank a cup of tea and then drove back to Catworth to complete their day's rabbit catching. These were Herbert's own words: 'Even my cap got soaked and it was still on my head.' Shortly after that event, in the winter of 1979, Herbert and his companion came to my house. They had been out ferreting rabbits at Molesworth and they had lost a ferret. Herbert assured me that it was a six hole sett and they had blocked all the holes securely. He said, 'It will be all right until tomorrow so if you can help us get it, will you meet us outside the Cross Keys about nine?' I said, yes I would be there. While we were talking my wife had been giving the two of them tea.

Next morning we met as arranged and proceeded up what had been the Molesworth Clopton road. Just before we reached the airfield perimeter fence we stopped and walked across one field and there were the blocked holes. The terrier I had with me sniffed around the holes and at one of them she stood and cocked her head very knowingly. I unblocked the hole and out walked the ferret. Herbert picked it up and that was that.

Now, I knew the farmer who owned that land. He had purchased the farm some five years previously and he was known to be none too friendly towards trespassers so as we walked along I remarked to Herbert that I hoped that he had permission to be on that land. He replied very seriously, 'Oh yes, Albert, permission was given to me to come here ferreting whenever I liked.' Then, as a kind of afterthought he added, 'Of course, it was some time ago because it was before the war and the 'drome wasn't here then.' I did not think that was too bad, considering the war had started some forty years before.

Another little incident that Herbert related to me was about the time when he was on land that was owned and farmed by the Co-op. Herbert said, 'I had caught five rabbits and the ferret was still in the hole. I was in a ditch that was not deep enough to give me much cover and I heard a motor coming along the field track. Of course I knew that whoever it was, they were sure to see me, so I quickly hid the rabbits under grass and soil. Sure enough it was the farm manager in his Land Rover. Of course he saw me and stopped. His first words were, "So you are poaching again, Webb, and I intend to report you, so come out of that ditch." I stood up and said, "All right but I am not leaving until I get my ferret out of this hole." "Right," said the manager, "I can wait," and that was what he did.'

After a little while Herbert recovered his ferret. 'Right,' the manager said, 'Now get on your way and you will hear more about this.' Herbert commenced his journey towards home then, as soon as the manager had driven off, he hurried back to where he had left the five rabbits, got them out of the ditch and put them in his haversack. He had just got back onto open ground when he heard the Land Rover engine and bearing down on him once again was the manager. Herbert said it was no use trying to escape and of course, the first words he said were, 'Empty your bag, Webb,' which he did and out came the five rabbits. 'Now,' said the manager,' I have you dead to rights.' Herbert said, 'Then I had an idea. I weighed about nine stone, he must have weighed about fifteen, but I stood up and hoped I looked big and impressive and I said, "Now you listen to me, the missus and me are both members of the Co-op and we get the Divi the same as you do and I reckon it also makes us part owners of this land, so you go and report me," and I picked up the five rabbits, put them in my bag and walked away; and do you know, Albert, I never heard another word.'

Charlie King

Before the last war I had only met Charlie King while he was the landlord of the Mermaid which was the public house at Ellington, a village beside the A14 road between Huntingdon and Thrapston. After the war Charlie was still the landlord of the Mermaid and I was to get to know him very well indeed. Charlie was not a very big man physically, I suppose five feet seven or thereabouts, slender in build with a wispy moustache but tremendously wiry and active and a mind like a computer. I never recall any time when Charlie was lost for words. Charlie told me once that his heaviest weight had never exceeded ten stone two pounds.

In the very late 1940s I was invited by a farmer who lived at Spaldwick to go with him to a shoot at Ellington. This shoot was over almost the whole parish of Ellington attended by most of the local farmers and their friends. We met of course at the Mermaid. The first item was countless half cups of coffee, the empty half of the cup being filled with rum. Never having been a well practised consumer of alcohol I had no intention of keeping up with those practised consumers, one of which was Bert Sharman, an old gamekeeper who during the war was in the Home Guard. One evening after imbibing heavily in the Catworth Fox Bert had staggered out onto the A604 road (now the A14) and stood in the road with his loaded rifle. The first vehicle that came along the road was an army staff car; it did not slow down so Bert put a 303 bullet through the radiator. In his own words to me, 'Lad, that sure stopped them.' Of course Bert was arrested and spent the night in a police cell. The following day his employer had to bail him out before they could carry out a day's shooting. Now, how could I compete with confirmed drinkers of that calibre?

Eventually we took to the fields. I was carrying my gun and walking with the beaters. Before each drive Charlie King, who was carrying a single barrelled twelve bore shotgun, would brief each beater by pointing his single barrel at them and instructing them as to where he wished them to go. Being briefed thus, I moved off with Ron Gray, a man my own age whom I knew very well. I said to Ron, 'Does Charlie ever load that old gun?' Ron replied, 'Of course he does; it is loaded now and the hammer cocked.' I thought at that moment, 'Whatever have I got myself into by coming here?' but I survived the day and avoided most of the fifty parts coffee with fifty parts rum in the evening.

If you are curious about the date, it was the night on which one of our up and coming heavyweight boxers fought an American named Joe Baksi at Wembley and Baksi broke our man's jaw in the fifth round. I know because in my rum-influenced state I was foolish enough to bet Jack Smith, a bookmaker who was a guest gun, £2 that our man would win. We listened to the fight in the kitchen in the Mermaid on the radio. That was another lesson on misplaced patriotism.

So as I progressed in my occupation of gamekeeping, I came to know Charlie better and better and the more I was in his company the more I realised what a remarkable person he was. He was landlord of the Mermaid public house; he was a part time chimney sweep, a part time gamekeeper; he farmed on some land adjacent to the wartime airfield of Kimbolton; he could be found carrying out the duties of a beater on a shoot day anywhere within ten miles of his home. I can recall the day when we had a good day at the partridges at Abbots Ripton in, I believe, 1960. Charlie had been beating all day and the bag was just over one hundred and fifty brace of partridge. At the end of the day all the game was laid out on the lawn and his Lordship, Lord de Ramsey, said, 'Right, King, you are the oldest beater, you will be photographed with the game.' In a second Charlie replied, 'Yes, my Lord, you know I came here beating before you were born and it is likely that I shall be coming here beating after you have gone.' But he was wrong. Lord de Ramsey still survives but Charlie is gone. I believe Charlie was eighty-two shortly after that day.

On another occasion when I was in charge of beaters we had to cross a brook at Leighton Bromswold. There was five or six feet depth of water and it was eighteen feet or so in width. The only way across was walking on a tree trunk that had been put across for just that purpose. When Charlie saw that trunk he said, 'I am not walking across that,' so after a short debate, I said, 'Right, Charlie, you are going over even if I have to carry you over.' In a moment he said, 'Right, that's it.' He then threw his stick over the brook and jumped on my back pick-a-back fashion. As I carried him over he said, 'If I go in you go in.' Of course we crossed all right. Charlie entertained a lot of people by telling the story of how he crossed the brook.

During our talking sessions Charlie told me that as a young man he had been a sawyer in a sawpit and he was always in the pit which meant that he did the hardest work. The saws they used only cut on the downward stoke so all the person on top did was pull the saw back up in preparation for the downward cut.

Charlie assured me that once for a wager he ate at one sitting twelve raw herrings and on another occasion he ate a four pound pork pie. He was allowed two half pints of beer to help wash the pork pie down. At Scott's timber yard at Thrapston Charlie carried five hundredweight of timber on his back and that was a gambling affair, a number of local persons being involved in the betting, also in the weighing and witnessing of the event. I would believe that carrying the five hundredweight of timber was easier than eating the herrings or the pork pie.

Charlie assured me that he once carried on his back ninety-nine rabbits across the fields from Brampton Wood to the Mermaid at Ellington and he had to stay in bed for the next four days. The weight would be in the region of three hundred pounds and the distance a mile or just over. Possible but improbable (my opinion).

I do know that Charlie was an expert caller of foxes especially of dog foxes. If I had have been born a dog fox Charlie's imitation of a vixen's scream at the time of the mating season would have fooled me. He told me that the highest number that he ever called and killed in one night was six, all dog foxes. This I know to be the truth.

A couple of my friends were Tom Jarvis and his wife Joan. They lived and worked at Salome Wood Lodge in the parish of Leighton Bromswold. Tom's father and mother also lived some two hundred yards distant. One night in 1953 Tom's mother became ill with a strangulated hernia and was taken to the County Hospital at Huntingdon. During the next day I saw Tom and he asked me if I would take him and Joan to see his mother on that evening. Of course I said yes and in the early evening I picked them up in my van and we went to the hospital. Our route took us right by the Mermaid. On our return journey Tom said, 'We cannot pass Charlie twice without calling in for a drink,' so we stopped outside the Mermaid. Tom said, 'You and Joan go in; I am going to the gents first.' The gents was through a farm gate behind the pub. Joan and I went in through the front door, closing it behind us. There were just a couple of persons and Charlie in the tap room. We exchanged Good evenings but Charlie did not reply; he just looked at us and then looked away. Of course he knew both of us very well. I asked him if we could have some drinks. He ignored my request. It was becoming difficult; then the door opened and in walked Tom. The change was instant. Charlie was behind the bar and poured out two pints of beer and a Guinness. When I laid money on the counter he refused it; he gave the counter a mighty blow with his fist and just said, 'Damn it, how easy it is to be bloody well wrong.' I believe he thought Joan and I were out for the evening.

Charlie also assured me that before he was married he had made a living with a travelling boxing booth taking on all comers of close to his own weight. He said there were some very rough persons about in those days and it was very easy to get a good hiding.

I have written about the next little incident before but it will be all right to tell it again. This was told to me by Frank Dickens and it was after the last war. Frank was head gamekeeper on the Kimbolton Estate. Frank said, 'It was after tea and I was up on the airfield when I saw a lot of smoke in the area of the two fields that Charlie farmed so I cycled along the perimeter track and when I got there the fire was almost out but I walked into what had been a field of barley. In the field was Charlie King and he looked very hot and bothered. At different points were heaps of smouldering corn that had obviously been in sacks so I said to Charlie, "Whatever has happened?" and this is what he said. "My son and I

74

A shoot day in Grove Wood, Hamerton

combined the field. My son went to Ellington towing the combine and he will be coming back with a trailer to pick up the corn and a bloody old fool pulled his fags and matches out, struck the match, lit his fag, threw the match down and in a second the straw was on fire and I couldn't put it out." Of course I said at once, "What has happened to the one who did such a foolish trick?" Charlie stroked his moustache both ways and replied, "Oh, that was me; I was the bloody old fool."'

Charlie always stated that he did keep the Mermaid because he always spent all the profit and two pounds besides. I believe he was referring to each week.

When Charlie was beating with me at Hamerton and was in his eighty-fifth year I would say to him, 'Now, Charles, you stay in the middle of the beating line because it will be a bit easier for you; there won't be so much walking for you,' but he would just reply,

'No, I'll be OK on the outside; you put some of the older ones in the middle.' Of course he was usually the oldest beater by at least ten years.

A truly remarkable character, faithful to his friends, generous to all and sundry, he never got out of line when beating and quickly put anyone right who did.

In 1967 he was taken ill and died on the longest day, 21 June. He was eighty-nine years of age.

I felt very privileged to be one of the bearers when he was buried.

Jack Engledow

It was 1955 when I first made the acquaintance of Jack Engledow. This is how it came about. One afternoon a half-ton Ford van stopped outside my house. A man got out and walked in through the front gate. He was a tall man, well built, with very rugged features, dressed in working men's clothes. He walked with a pronounced limp and smoked a pipe. I met him at the door. He looked straight at me and said, 'You are Albert Spring,' and I replied, 'Yes, that is my name.' He held his right hand out and said, 'I am Jack Engledow.' We shook hands.

He entered my house and at my invitation he sat down. This is what he said. 'I am employed by Chivers at Histon and am their pest operator; I have been told that you are a good hand at training a dog for the shooting field. Now my boss Mr Stanley Chivers is obtaining a puppy in the very near future and he sent me to enquire if you would be willing to train it for him.' All this was said with a very pronounced Norfolk accent interrupted only by puffs at his pipe.

It transpired that there was a man employed by Chivers who went to school at Hamerton; his mother still lived in the village of Hamerton and he had been talking about my ability as a trainer of dogs. Possibly a case of mistaken praise, but after a cup of tea and an hour or so talking I had come to the conclusion that Jack was a man after my own heart who also had a great knowledge of the ways of the wild. He also showed a great interest in my terriers without divulging any informaton about his own special activities. Before he left we agreed that I would consider the training of the proposed puppy for Mr Stanley Chivers but I would have to talk with that gentleman to find out exactly what his requirements were. Before he left Jack gave me his address, 7 Villa Road, Histon, and phone number. He had bought the house that he lived in.

Some six weeks later I received a letter from Jack to say that Mr Stanley Chivers had obtained a puppy and intended to visit me on a certain day at a certain time. If it was not suitable for me I could phone Jack and change it. I did not phone

At the time and day Mr Stanley Chivers and his wife arrived at my house. We shook hands, my wife made a pot of tea and we talked about the puppy. Much to my surprise Mr Stanley said, 'I have the puppy with me in the car and I wish you to have it now,' and he went out to his car and returned with the puppy. It was eight weeks of age, a pretty little bitch looking like an Irish red setter pup.

I explained that taking on the training at that age would cost a considerable amount of money because it would take over a year before the training was complete. He said, 'That is all right,' and gave me an envelope. He said, 'There are fifty pounds in cash; tell Engledow when you need more and he will tell me.'

Please bear in mind that in 1955 it was possible to purchase a fully trained labrador or springer spaniel for forty pounds or thereabouts.

We talked for some time and he told me that the puppy was out of a pure bred Irish red setter bitch and the sire was a yellow labrador dog that travelled the county mating in-season bitches. He added these remarks: 'I chose this puppy deliberately and I wish you to train her to hunt and point or set and then when I have prepared myself to shoot I can say, right, put it up now, then if I hit it she will fetch it for me,' and then he said, 'Oh, and her name will be Miss Bunting.'

Over a year passed and Jack Engledow came over to see how Miss Bunting was progressing every couple of months or so. The funny thing is that Miss Bunting eventually hunted, pointed or set, flushed when told and retrieved. She was also pretty. It was like a man having a very pretty wife who could also cook.

The only conclusion that I could come to was that the pup was listening when Mr Stanley had instructed me on all those points. I think it was a little bit uncanny to be so successful.

On his visits Jack told me a lot about himself. He was a native of Stiffkey on the Norfolk coast. Stiffkey was notorious for the scandal about the then Vicar of Stiffkey and a certain lady named Barbara Harris. That was some time around 1930; it was all in the *News of the World.*

Jack and I were soon visiting each other very regularly on the several thousands of acres that were owned by Chivers Ltd. There were a lot of opportunities for terrier work after fox, rats and rabbits. There was also a lot of game, i. e., pheasants, partridges and hares. This was brought about entirely by Jack's efforts at the controlling of both predatory mammals and predatory birds. The Chivers family did not make a practice of organized shooting, possibly having a couple or three part-days each season. There was a lot of land that a shot was never fired on from one year's end to the next except by Jack and a number of characters who poached a few for the pot.

Chivers at one time grew all their own soft fruits and vegetables that they required for their canning industry. They also specialised in breeding pedigree work horses, cattle, pigs, and poultry. Chivers pedigree Light Sussex poultry were famous over the whole of Great Britain and in my time all of the poultry units were controlled by the redoubtable Miss Bacon. Now it was Jack's job to protect all those projects to the best of his ability. Jack's wife was named Mabel and a very sweet and kind person she was. For a number of

Jack Engledow. Sorting his traps.

years, Mabel worked as charge-hand for Unwin's, the seeds specialists at Histon.

Jack was a very clever trapper of all predators. He was also a licensed trapper of bullfinches. He caught around five hundred of these pests each season. His traps were composed of six different compartments. In one of the compartments a live decoy bullfinch was confined and the other five were capable of catching one bird each at each setting. The reason for taking these birds was to protect the fruit trees when they were loaded with blossom. One bullfinch is capable of destroying forty-eight buds per minute. That is Ministry figures: Jack told me it was a very low estimate.

Jack was also an expert at trapping and poisoning moles. Of course Jack again had to have a Ministry licence to obtain the strychnine for this purpose. He told me that one eighth of a grain of strychnine was a lethal dose for a human being. The standard aspirin tablet weighs five grains so that gives us a good idea of how dangerous it is to use. Jack told me a number of stories that amused me so they may amuse any person who reads what I write.

Jack had one little trick if he was asked to catch a mole or rabbit or rat in someone's garden or buildings. Once he had set his traps to his own satisfaction he would turn to the person for whom he was doing the favour and ask them if they could fetch a tumbler part-filled with water for him. When this was brought to him, Jack in a very solemn manner would proceed to sprinkle a few spots of the water around the trapped area. If anyone asked why, Jack in the same solemn manner would reply that by doing that he was ensuring that the traps only caught what they were set to catch. Of course it got around Histon that Jack was a bit of a sorcerer as well as a good trapper. Anyhow, one day Mr Stanley Chivers requested his presence in his office and after the usual greetings Mr Stanley said, 'Now, Engledow, my sister has some trouble with rabbits in her garden; would you deal with them for her?'

Jack of course replied, 'Yes, Mr Stanley, of course I will.'

Then, as Jack turned to leave the office, Mr Stanley said to him, 'Oh, Engledow, and you can dispense with the mumbo jumbo business with the water because my sister has heard all about it.'

On another occasion one of the farm managers asked Jack to attend to some problem on one of the farms. Jack told him, 'Sorry, it will have to wait; I am very busy.'

The manager told Jack, 'Busy or not, you damn well get over there and attend to it.'

Jack got in his van, drove straight down to Mr Stanley's office and asked to see Mr Stanley. Mr Stanley asked Jack what was wrong. Jack told him what had happened; he also reminded Mr Stanley that he only took orders from the head office which he was then in because none of the managers had sufficient knowledge of his specialised work to give him orders. Jack never had any more trouble of that kind.

One year in the late 1950s they had trouble with starlings. They would come in great droves and take the pellets out of the wooden troughs that the free-range poultry were fed in. Jack was asked to do something about it so he constructed a number of wood and wire pens to fit over the troughs. The pens had funnel entrances and when the time was right the pens were placed over the troughs when they were full of food. Jack caught nine thousand starlings in three days. Jack cut off all the starlings' wings and sold them to Horace, friends at Wisbech. He received 2½*d.* per pair for them. The bodies he sold to a firm that manufactured artificial manure. They weighed twelve hundredweight and they paid Jack 12*s.* 6*d.* per hundredweight.

On another occasion at the poultry farm which was situated at Arbury on the outskirts of Histon, they had a large invasion of rats. It was Jack's job to deal with them. In his own words, it was not an easy proposition. The rats had an unlimited supply of good, i.e. poultry, food, both grain and pellets. The gin trap had been banned in 1958. All the poultry food was stored in a large old-fashioned thatched wooden barn. It was under this barn and under other buildings close by that the rats had their sleeping quarters so Jack made his plan. Close to the barn, right beside the main holes that the rats had made in the wooden barn, he dug holes each large enough to accommodate a cut of forty gallon barrel. Of course he covered each barrel top over with a board and a sprinkling of soil. It took him a week to complete the task. He also blocked all other holes with wire netting. Then, when the time was right, he half filled each sunken drum with water and after night fall he very quietly went and removed the cover from each of the drums. Then he nipped into the barn, pulled the door shut behind him and switched on the lights. There were literally hundreds of rats; they all scrambled for their escape holes and of course fell straight into the tanks half filled with water. The next morning Jack removed 503 rats from his home-made traps. He tried again two nights later and caught a further 315. One week later he caught a further 226 but on numerous occasions thereafter he did not take a single rat. In Jack's own words, the survivors had moved to a more welcome home, after losing 1024 of their friends and relatives.

Jack buried the dead rats in a hole he dug not too far away. He said the hole was full to within a foot from the top so he levelled it all up with soil. Six months later some architect was in the yard examining the barn with a plan of replacing it with a more modern building. He inadvertently walked onto the rats' grave and, in Jack's words, there was a real stink in more ways than one.

Now I will put you in the picture of what I know about Jack. He told me that the cause of his limp went back to when he was thirteen years of age. He was working in a cornfield with a number of other persons and entirely by accident he sustained a severe cut from a scythe on the back of his right leg exactly level with his knee joint. The cut had been sewn up by a doctor but some tendons or sinews must have been severed because that leg had never developed as it ought to have done. It was two and a half inches shorter than his left leg and the foot needed seven socks on it to match up to the other one. Of course, throughout the years Jack had taught himself to cope at all times with his disability, so much so that if he had to cross a deep ditch or any other difficult obstacle and I offered to help him he would say, 'No, keep out of my way; I would have to manage if I was on my own.'

Jack was a master of trapping with gin traps. He had an enormous number of these varying in jaw size from one and a half inches to six inches, so when the use of these traps was banned in England in 1958 he was almost completely lost, mainly because he had never set a snare to catch a rabbit or a fox in the whole of his life. Of course, at snaring I was the expert, so when Chivers Limited had trouble at Hardwick with foxes taking lambs, Jack straight away sent for me so I went over and I took a number of fox snares with me.

We went to Hardwick and surveyed the scene. During the day the ewes and their lambs were allowed to graze on a large field, then each evening they were shepherded into a sheltered field about six acres in size. It was completely enclosed by a hedge and also good sheep wire fencing on good posts. We went all the way round the wire fence and located five places where in our opinion a fox or foxes had entered the field by going under the wire. I set a snare at each of these places. Jack watched very carefully. I told him that I did not expect to catch a fox until the third night. Of course Jack knew why. He knew the ways of the fox. I had tea at Jack's house and came home.

On the fifth day I received a letter from Jack. This is how it was written. 'Morning one, not a snare touched, not a lamb touched. Morning two, not a snare touched, not a lamb touched. Morning three, dog fox in snare close to gate. It was the first snare we set. Another dog fox in third snare. We have reset snares, not a lamb touched. Morning four, in-whelp vixen in fourth snare we set.' A later letter stated that three more foxes had been caught. Of the six snares that we had set only one had failed to catch. The first snare we had set caught twice. Jack was so impressed that he straight away ordered one hundred snares. I told him he had caught snare fever.

Now, please understand it was extremely unlikely that more than one of the six foxes that were caught were doing the lamb killing. It does not work that way. If every fox was a lamb killer then it would be a very poor outlook for our flocks of sheep.

Jack owned a pure bred smooth-haired fox terrier bitch. She went everywhere with Jack and would not take any notice of any other person except Jack's wife Mabel. In 1960 this terrier had killed a total of seventy-one foxes underground single-handed, but she had sustained so many injuries that Jack would put a long strong cord on her collar and once the bitch had bayed, which meant that there was a fox in the drain or earth, he would coax the bitch out with the cord and his voice. He would then put a spoonful of dry gas in each hole, stop up all the holes securely usually using a sack part-filled with soil, and of course the fox usually died with its nose on the gas. Jack knew the exact amount of gas to use.

One day Jack was after rabbits. He had his terrier with him and he suddenly realised that the bitch was missing. He eventually located her. She had found a fox in an enlarged rabbit burrow and, according to Jack, there was one hell of a battle going on. Of course, Jack started digging and eventually he got down to them by which time all was quiet. The bitch was still alive but in a terrible state. The fox was dead, the bitch had killed her seventy-second fox, and it was to be her last because in spite of the best treatment that the vet could provide, the bitch survived for a further three weeks and then passed away.

Of course, Jack without a terrier was like a cricketer without his arms. At that time I had a good two-year-old terrier dog that was already entered to fox and so of course I made a present of that terrier to Jack. It was a funny business, the hardest part being to persuade Jack that I was not feeling sorry for him. He detested what he called Charity.

He called the dog Tim, although that was not his original name. In fact, in Jack's own words, he changed everything except the dog's nationality. After Tim got used to Jack and Jack got used to Tim everything was fine again. Tim was a true working terrier. He never bayed underground unless he was up to his fox and then he would stay as long as anyone wished but he would if called leave his fox and return to the surface. Some four years later Jack told me that he had taken three hundred and fifty foxes with Tim and had only had cause to take Tim to the vet once, but, he added, Tim does not kill foxes.

Some ten years later when Tim was old I gave Jack another young dog. Of course its name had to be Tim and that one lasted until Jack retired.

For a great number of years Jack had arthritis in his hip and in the 1960s we often visited Madingley Hall for the purpose of killing foxes that resided there in the shelter of the woodlands surrounding the Hall. Madingley Hall was used by the senior medical staff of that famous hospital at Cambridge (Addenbrooke's). Madingley Hall was the staff's hall of recreation and Doctor Dick, a senior surgeon, also rented the sporting rights of the Park and so Jack helped Doctor Dick with the predator problems. Jack's limp became more and more pronounced and one day the doctor said to Jack, 'Now then, Jack, why don't you let me put you a new hip joint in?' and Jack very politely replied, 'Doctor, when I see a person to whom you have given a new hip joint walk along the street without two sticks, I will let you do mine.' Of course, at that time the joint replacement business was in its infancy.

Of course time takes its toll and in the late 1970s Jack retired. A couple of years later Mabel suffered a severe stroke and died in the early 1980s. Shortly afterwards Jack had to have an operation on his eyes and shortly after that a joint replacement on his hip. All these things took their toll on him and in 1986 he expressed the wish to visit his birthplace once more so I drove down to Stiffkey with Jack as my passenger. It was funny: as we got closer to our destination Jack would say, 'Stop here, Albert, I want to show you something.' We could not stop as the road was narrow and there was a terrific amount of traffic in both directions. We arrived at Stiffkey and Jack showed me the house in which he was born and spent his boyhood. Then we visited the churchyard at Stiffkey. The churchyard was very tidy of course. We lingered for some time especially beside the graves of his parents. Jack just stood there and puffed at his pipe; his face was void of any expression at all. I walked away and left him with his thoughts. I would think his thoughts were very private.

We visited Blakeney Point and Jack pointed out all the places where he used to shoot wildfowl when he was young. We visited Cley Next the Sea and had lunch with a cousin of Jack's. I never knew her surname. Jack just said, 'Albert, meet my cousin Mary,' and to Mary he said, 'Meet my friend Albert.' We had a very good lunch and Mary was such a pleasant person.

We visited Morston and Greencroft and we stopped in a gateway to a farm and Jack told me that it was that farm which had been owned by a gentleman named Williamson who had written that very popular book *Tarka the Otter* while he lived and farmed there.

We were thinking about commencing our return journey when Jack again shouted, 'Stop!' which I did as quickly and safely as I could. Jack said, 'Drive back to that bungalow.' This I did and there was a tall old man working in the garden. He and Jack had attended the same school. Of course we were soon in the bungalow and how I wished that I could have got their conversation on a tape recorder. It was carried on in broad Norfolk brogue and went on for almost an hour. That was our last call and we returned to Histon. It was a day I will never forget and for Jack his last visit ever to his birthplace. Of course he would remember it to the end of his days.

Jack deteriorated rapidly and became incapable of looking after himself effectively and finished his days in the Tower Hospital at Ely.

When I was out in the fields with Jack he would often say, 'Albert, the only thing that I envy is your ability in getting over fences and ditches.'

I am glad that I met Jack Engledow and enjoyed so many happy days with him.

Joe Morris

It was very shortly after the 1939–45 war that I first met Joe. He was a very rugged, sturdy type of man, married with two daughters. He was underkeeper at Lord Brassey's estate at Apethorpe in Northamptonshire. The headkeeper was Harry Goodson. Joe loved his pipe and although it was often unlit it was never far away from his mouth. He is as fond of his pipe today as he was when I first met him. His nickname is Smokey Joe.

He left the Apethorpe Estate in the 1950s and took on the job as single handed gamekeeper at the Holme Estate which is situated on the east side of the A1 road, a couple of miles south of Norman Cross. He was a good honest keeper but was also a very stubborn person. The sporting was rented out to a syndicate and as long as

Joe showed them plenty of game he could have it all his own way. It was a very good area for wild game, being light Fen soil and free of gapes which is a killer among wild and hand reared game.

Of course, there were a lot of foxes in the area and Joe often came to me to help him deal with these pests so we got to know each other very well. We did a lot of good work with my terriers on that shoot, then we would share a pot of tea at Joe's house and Joe would tell me all about the local poachers. He knew them all and they all knew Joe. There were a number of poachers who netted pheasants at night with drop nets. Most of these nets were made of very fine hemp usually about twelve feet by thirty-six feet. I have one in my house and that is the size. A slender wooden pole twelve feet long was threaded through the ends of the net and then the two men dragged the net over sugar beet or carrot crops keeping the front end some four feet high and allowing the rear end to drag lightly over the crop, whatever it was. The moment a bird flushed under the net the whole net was dropped and whatever happened to be underneath was quickly killed and put in the bag.

Joe told me that one night he was out on the Fen and he heard an old cock pheasant fly up out of a field of carrots so he stood and listened for a little while and he heard another. He said, 'I knew what was going on; it was somebody netting but the old cock birds were too crafty for them and flew up before they were under the net.' Joe said, 'I had my torch and so I stalked them very quietly and I got within twenty-five yards of them before they knew I was there. There were three of them,' Joe said, 'I put my light on and shouted, "This is the police!" But they ran in three different directions so I ran after one of them and he jumped into one of the main dykes. The water was some four feet deep and ten feet wide. He did not show himself on the other side so I knew he was keeping quiet in the water under the bank so I just gets me pipe out and lights up. I smoked away for nearly an hour and then I said, "I am going now so you had better get on home before you catch your death of cold."' Joe said, 'A week later it was gossiped about in the local pubs and they did not say anything complementary about me; in fact they called me a name that suggested my mother had never been married.'

Joe recovered the net and a sack of dead pheasants at first light the following day.

Since writing the previous page I have talked with an old friend who was an expert night netter of pheasants in his younger days and he informed me that the net could be anything in size from twelve feet by thirty up to eighteen feet by ninety. The mesh must be four inches so that the birds could get their head through but not their body. The same man also told me that in 1947 he was asked to catch a number of hen pheasants alive for egg laying and he and two companions netted three hundred in one night. They killed the cock birds; all they had to do was feel for the spurs on their legs. The hens they put in sacks and took away alive. He said that as they drove home with their loot the workmen were just going to work; it was just getting daylight.

The reader may think that I have some strange friends. Well, I have some of them who only visit me during the hours of darkness and the more daring ones make a very careful reconnaissance of the area before they call on me.

We must return to Joe after he retired from full time employment. As a gamekeeper he still did part time work for several people. He would do a job like catching rabbits where they had built up to a high density or trapping rats, stoats, carrion, crows, etc., on farms that were not large enough to warrant the employment of a full time keeper.

In 1988 or 89 Joe was looking after some land on which a lot of young trees had been planted. These young trees were planted on all sides of a small wood on the top of a hill. The wood is known as the Roundhills and it was a very popular draw for the local pack of foxhounds, for the simple reason that they usually found a fox in it.

One day the hounds and their master and the huntsman and a

large number of mounted followers were intent on drawing the Roundhills but when they reached the gate that barred their way to the field that surrounded the wood it was securely held closed by a stout chain and padlock and leaning on the gate smoking his pipe was Joe. The master eyed the chain and padlock and then Joe. He enquired very politely why the gate was locked and on whose order it had been locked. Joe replied that his boss had given him the order and that he had carried it out. The next question was why? Joe replied that it was easy to see that all the ground around the wood was planted with young trees and the people who owned the land would not allow horses to trample them down so entry was forbidden. This conversation had been carried out in an amicable way between the Master of Fox Hounds and Joe, but then a local farmer who was a staunch supporter of the hunt intruded into the talking. He said rather loudly, 'Come on, Joe, we have always hunted the Roundhills, so let us through.' On this remark Joe quickly asked the Master to excuse him for one moment and, turning to the person concerned, he said in a very clear voice, 'You may not be aware that when I am talking to the Master it is very rude of his bloody monkey to interrupt.' Of course this did not help matters in any way at all and so the hunt was turned away but Joe is no longer in charge so they may be welcome again in the very near future.

Fred Whitwell

Fred was a cousin to my mother on her mother's side of the family so I had known him all my life but it was not until 1946 and 1947 that we became better acquainted. We certainly had some enjoyable times together.

Fred owned and maintained a small fleet of lorries and he moved a lot of merchandise around the country, mainly bricks and sugar beet. He was in the right area for these commodities, being based at Whittlesey.

Fred was a very straight dealer and honest in all his business dealings and so was very well liked and respected but of course there was another side to his life. He loved the ways of the wild and again he was in the right area, the edge of the deep Fenlands.

Fred knew all the calls of the wild geese and the whistle of the widgeon and other duck and he could imitate them all as nearly perfectly as it was possible to do. Very few people knew of his skill and knowledge because he always or nearly always operated entirely alone. I believe in the whole of his life he only had but one real comrade in all his activities among the wild fowl, the game and the fish. Fred plaited perfect eel hives; these were made of split willow wands and were a work of art and very effective. Fred caught tons of eels in hives and no one about knew what he was up to. He made nets and netted the Fen drains, catching fish by the hundredweight, all of which were in central or Leadenall market by the following morning. He always succeeded because he knew exactly when the conditions were right and that was the secret to his success. He even owned and often used an eel gleave. Of course these were illegal, but Fred would give a little chuckle and say with a twinkle in his eye, 'It's only illegal if you are caught using it.'

Fred would often go to the coast and gather samphire, a very edible type of seaweed. He always knew where to find it and he always knew where to get the best price for it.

Fred knitted all sorts of nets, drag or drop nets for pheasants. He knew the best material to use and he knew the best nights to get the best results when making use of them. I was talking with his one and only known comrade after Fred's funeral at Whittlesey who told me that he worked mostly at night with Fred for over forty years and that Fred always succeeded because they only operated when Fred decided that the wind and the water and the light were right. He also said, 'I never had any other true friend but Fred Whitwell and it is too late now to find another.' He said, 'Fred and I shot geese and duck by the hundred; we netted pheasants by the hundred and netted fish by the ton and only God knows how many eels we caught in hives that Fred made and Fred always knew where to get rid of what we got.' He then added, 'And only Fred's wife and my wife ever saw us together; it was usually dark.' We shook hands and he walked away. I do not know his name.

Now I will tell a few of my own experiences with Fred Whitwell. Fred and I, although distantly related, did not really get together until after the war and I had been wildfowling a few times. Then one Sunday Fred and his wife Ann visited my mother. I happened to be in my mother's house at the time and we got talking to one another. Our talk was all about ferrets, dogs, game, birds, wild fowl, hares, rabbits and pigeon, and in spite of Fred not letting any secrets slip past his tongue I knew that he knew a lot more about the ways of the wild than he was telling me at that time.

I was invited to his house and I accepted the invitation and so it progressed, first at his house and then at mine, and slowly but surely Fred talked and showed me his tackle as he described his traps and nets. Up to that time I had never seen an eel hive or a proper drag or drop net or a four-inch gin trap with a few grains of maize glued onto the plate so that when the trap was set in nine inches or so of water a mallard taking a peck at the glued maize would be caught by the head and quickly drowned. Fred's one word of caution was, 'Never set that trap if there are any swans in the area.' He chuckled and said, 'Some people object if they see a swan trying to take off with a four-inch gin trap on its beak.' When he chuckled, I bet he was thinking of the last time that happened.

So we progressed. I visited Fred and we accounted for a tremendous number of foxes on farms where Fred had permission to take them. Fred shot pigeon and joined us on organized hare shoots. He was really over the moon when at one hare shoot at Winwick he killed twenty-five hares to his own gun on one drive alone. The total bag on that one drive was six short of three hundred.

One of Fred's favourite sports was standing in a wood and waiting for pigeon to flight into the wood to roost. He was an above average shot and always made a good average of kills per shots fired. Fred and I and a number of other friends had a great number of enjoyable evenings together after we had been out shooting. We would get into the person's house closest to where we had been out shooting and out would come the whisky and Tia Maria and we would all have a drink together before going our separate ways, just like the life of Riley.

It was a great shock and loss to his family and friends when Fred was stricken with an incurable illness that quickly killed him. He had not lived to pension age.

Danny Dunmore

Danny Dunmore lived with his sister Kitty at Old Weston in the 1920s and early 1930s. A huge man without being fat, he had one good eye and one glass eye. He had served in the Navy when there were still a number of sailing ships in service.

He repaired cycles, I mean the two-wheeled cycles that we rode in that day and age. He also delivered newspapers in Old Weston and to a number of other villages riding a large Norton motor cycle for that purpose.

He was also the self appointed manager of Old Weston football team. One Saturday Winwick football team played Old Weston at Old Weston and during the match the referee gave a decision against the Old Weston Team that Danny did not agree with so Danny charged onto the pitch, knocked the referee to the ground with one mighty blow of his fist, picked up his whistle and refereed the remainder of the match himself. All this happened without a stoppage of play. That is the only really interesting incident that I can recall about Danny.

Vic Banks

It was in the mid 1950s that I met Vic. He and his brother owned and farmed a medium sized farm in Bedfordshire. Vic loved to go shooting. He was not adverse to a day foxhunting or otter hunting but his greatest love outside his family was and still is (and this is January 1993) beer drinking. Vic just loved his beer but he was intelligent enough not to let it interfere with his business of farming.

One evening in the 1960s Oscar Jordan and I walked into the Crown Public House at Little Staughton. We had been disposing of an old vixen and her litter of cubs on the farm owned by Vic and his brother. The Crown was kept by Mrs Guy. This lady was rumoured to have occult powers; that may not be the right word but she was often referred to as a witch. When we entered there was a full grown fox sitting on one end of the bar and a large white hob ferret inspecting the customers' beer.

The fox was a present from Oscar to Mrs Guy when we had been at the same sort of job a year previous. Of course at that time it was a cub and Mrs Guy had requested it from Oscar and she had made an excellent job of rearing and taming it.

When we entered the bar, Mrs Guy said to the fox, 'Make yourself scarce. The sods that murdered your mother have just come in.' The fox dived off the bar and was gone. The ferret just carried on with his inspection. Vic was playing cards with three other people; I believe they were playing nap. Vic glanced at Mrs Guy and that lady served us with a pint of beer each. We drank and a minute or two later we got in a word or two with Vic. He asked us if we had been successful and the answer was yes.

The conversation progressed and we were invited to partake of more beer which I refused.

Vic said, 'Don't you like beer, Albert?'

I replied, 'Of course I do, but I am twelve miles from home.'

Then he said, 'I understand, of course, but I love it; I shall drink as much as I can tonight and tomorrow morning I shall feel bloody awful but by God I will enjoy it tonight,' and that was and is to this day Vic's attitude to beer.

J. D. Vervoorn

This man was a Dutchman. I met him in Holland in September 1944. I knew him as Hans. He was an eighteen-year-old medical student, also a very active member of the Dutch wartime Resistance. I was a sergeant in the paratroops. I was in command of a plane-load of paratroops when we were shot down by German anti-aircraft fire. This happened in the Opheasden, Kesteren, and Dodeward area close to the River Waal.

Hans Vervoorn was one of the first Dutchmen to approach us. We had suffered a number of casualties, both dead and injured, so we were extremely glad of the assistance we received from Hans and his brave comrades. Hans was the most valuable to us because he could speak very good English. In the following week I was to value his knowledge of the area and the people more and more. He was a very brave and resourceful man. I was dressed in a civilian suit and rode a cycle in his company, all of which were supplied by members of the Resistance. When we were halted by a German patrol or sentry he and his friend Harri seemed to be capable of talking so convincingly that we were always allowed to proceed on our way. Then Hans would remark as we cycled away, 'They will never know how close they were to being killed.' He meant the Germans of course.

Eventually with the help of Hans and his comrades we escaped to territory that was in the hands of the Allied forces. I was not to see Hans in person again until 1991 although we did communicate through the post for a number of years after the war.

Hans had qualified in the field of medicine and eventually became a professor in that field. He worked for the Dutch

Professor J.D. Vervoorn from the Netherlands.

Government and for most of his working life was stationed in the Dutch colonies. We no longer communicated.

About 1987 Hans had retired and was living in Amersfoort in Holland. Of course he had married and had a family of two girls and one boy, all of whom were then in their twenties. At this time Hans decided once again to communicate with his English friends of 1944 and of course I was the first person that he contacted through the Airborne journal (*The Pegasus*) so once again we were in regular communication. In 1991 my son Philip and I spent a full week as the guests of the Vervoorn family. We were entertained as though we were royalty and we met all the surviving members of the Dutch wartime Resistance.

Harri Tomason, one of the valiant men who assisted us in 1944, was a very sick man and died on 26 September 1991. This is what Hans told me in his letters: Harri made all his own arrangements for his own funeral; he also asked Hans to speak for him on that day. He said to Hans, 'Be very careful what you say, because I will be in my coffin listening to you.'

This was another one of Hans' stories. In the 1950s he was practising as a doctor in Ghana for his Government and his salary was very low but he was allowed to carry out a limited amount of private work. One day he was asked to visit a lady by her husband and it was in a very, very poor area. When he arrived at the hut the lady was in labour and had been in that state for some time so he decided that he would have to carry out a caesarean operation. This was duly carried out and mother and child survived. Several weeks later Hans was summoned to the local Administration Office and was informed by the Administration Officer that he had received a complaint that he, Hans Vervoorn, had insulted a certain lady by failing to make a charge for performing a successful caesarean operation on her. The lady said that by not making a charge Hans had implied that she was so poor that she could not afford to pay.

The officer advised Hans to visit the lady and apologise which he did. The lady accepted the apology on the condition that he accepted a fee, so it was agreed there and then that the lady would pay Hans whatever she could afford. She agreed to pay Hans a fee of four chicken eggs in instalments of one egg per week for four weeks, Hans said, and her dignity was satisfied.

Bill

Bill was a dog, a terrier standing twelve inches at the shoulders and weighing some fourteen pounds, very sturdy and strong. His colour was white with tan markings on his head and ears. He was a very good looking working terrier with a good broken coat of hair to give him good protection in the cold weather. (The term broken coat is used for a dog when its coat is too coarse to be called smooth and not coarse enough to be called rough.

Bill was born in 1951. His mother was my bitch Pickle. I had purchased Pickle from a Mr S. G. Hallet at Charlton Mackrel in Somerset. She was a good bitch for work. His sire was my dog Sprig, a very good dog for work but very surly in his behaviour. We always said that the only time Sprig wagged his tail was when he was looking at a fox.

When Bill was some eight weeks of age he was sold to a young lady named Ruby who lived at Finedon in Northamptonshire. We did warn Ruby that we did not think that Bill would be a very suitable dog for town life and if at any time he got too unruly and out of hand we would have him back.

Everything went along beautifully with Bill until he was just under one year old but one evening Ruby was taking him for a walk on a lead along the street at Finedon. The lead was held rather loosely by Ruby. Unfortunately as they walked along some dear old lady stood at her door calling her cat, possibly for its evening meal. The door was three steps above the pavement and was open. The cat went up the steps. Bill saw it and went after it. Bill got through the door as quick as the cat and killed the cat in the small hallway. The dear old lady was very annoyed and reported the incident to the police. Ruby had no alternative except getting rid of Bill.

We now had Bill back. He was a beautiful terrier to look at but never at any time did we show Bill as a Jack Russell type of terrier at any of the working terrier shows. I as a gamekeeper was only interested in Bill as a working terrier.

As long as Bill was alive Ruby came to see him, always bringing a present: a new collar, a new food bowl, a new drinking bowl, a new lead, or a box of chocolates. Bill always made a fuss of her. Temperamentally Bill was near to being perfect. He was willing to kill rats, cats, hedgehogs and, given the opportunity, a pig once in a while. He would go to ground after fox or badger and was afraid of nothing, or if he was he never showed his fear.

He never turned away from another dog but he was never in the whole of his life involved in a fight with one. Bill knew all the children in the village and when the children played football or any other ball game on the green in front of my mother's house, Bill was always picked to play on one side or the other. To see him dribble a football was a splendid sight.

Only on one single occasion did Bill bite anyone. I will write about that in a little while.

We had decided that Bill would live in my mother's house with my mother. He had lived in Ruby's house and was house-trained and very clean in his habits. If anyone knocked on my mother's door at any time he would sniff at the door and if he recognised the smell as a friend he would wag his tail. If it was a stranger he would growl and he was never wrong. One day I went down to my mother's house and there was Bill hanging on to the leg of a coloured man. There were items like scarves, neckties, tablecloths, etc. scattered over the road. Bill was growling and hanging on. The man was swearing I believe in several different languages and trying to get free. Of course I grabbed Bill and persuaded him to let go. The man was very angry and uttered a number of threats against Bill, my mother and myself but he soon picked up his goods, climbed into his van and was gone. We never saw him again.

I asked my mother what had happened and this is what she told me. 'There was a knock on the door. Bill took a sniff and growled. I opened the door a little way and saw this man. He was polite when he asked me if I wished to buy any of his goods but when I said no he became very persistent and so I asked him to go away and I tried to close the door but he put his foot in it and without thinking I shouted Bill and that was it. Bill had his ankle in his mouth and then you came on the scene. Whatever would have happened if you had not turned up, I do not know.' I believed my mother's description of what had happened.

At the back of my mother's house was a large garden at the top end of which was a large orchard. Here was a clothes line on which my mother hung her washing. Also in the orchard was a large white sow with her litter of piglets. One day my mother, when taking her washing up to the orchard to hang it on the clothes line, failed to close the back door of the house and also left the small gate between the garden and the orchard open. Of course Bill took the opportunity and went up to the orchard. He saw the piglets and straight away attacked them. The piglets were some seven weeks old. Bill grabbed one by its middle and of course the sow chased Bill through the gate down the garden and into the house. Bill still had the piglet in his mouth and the sow was intent on getting Bill into her mouth. The sow weighed approximately five hundred pounds. They knocked everything over in the kitchen and Bill escaped through the back door and up into the orchard. He dropped the piglet which of course was dead and made his escape. The most serious aspect of all this was that my mother could have been injured very easily so I made arrangements for Bill to go to the Oakley Hunt Kennels but my mother refused to let him go when the time came for his departure.

Opposite to my mother's house was a house named Rose Cottage. A man named Cooper lived there, an American serviceman based in England. His wife's name was Jenny, a German girl that Cooper had married while he was based in Germany. They had three children and a ginger tom cat. Bill was a regular guest in their house; the children and Jenny gave him all kinds of titbits. Bill always ignored the ginger tom cat.

Jenny was a nice person and a splendid cook and would often nip over to my mother's house to give some of her cookies to her. One day when on such a mission her cat followed her and sat on my mother's doorstep. Bill was in his own backyard; he must have taken a look through the open door that led to the street and observed the cat on his doorstep. He promptly attacked the cat and by the time Jenny got the front door open Bill was on his way to her house with the cat which was now dead in his mouth. Bill deposited the body on its own doorstep and trotted back home.

This caused a lot of tears but after a week or so Bill was again a welcome guest at the Coopers' in Rose Cottage.

One Saturday Jim Turner and I followed the local pack of fox-hounds. Of course we were travelling on the road in my van. We had Bill and another terrier in their travelling box with us. The hounds ran a fox to ground in a drain on the edge of the wartime aerodrome at Polebrook. Bill entered the drain after the fox. After about fifteen minutes Bill had pulled the fox so that the fox's head was clear of the drain. The huntsman despatched the fox using his humane killer. The hounds then fell on the fox and broke it up and after it was all over Bill jumped into the van and into his travelling box. He still had the fox's mask in his teeth.

Some people will say this is cruel and should be banned but if one gives a little thought to it all, the reason that it happens is mainly because the fox is, except the badger, the largest of our predatory animals and so is only preyed upon by man. In 1954 a neighbouring keeper came to my house. These are his own words. He said, 'Albert, I reckon I know where an old fox hangs out,' and so after a cup of tea we took Bill and his sister to have a look. We went into a field. It was grass and a fox or foxes had enlarged a rabbit burrow all right. The two main holes were some fifteen metres apart. We put a net on the farthest away hole and entered the terrier bitch in the other hole. The bitch did not get a chance to bay before she was backed out of the hole with a very nasty bite on her nose. Of course the bitch was not as big as Bill so I took Bill's collar off and in he went to be driven out just as quickly. The fox did not let go of Bill's muzzle until his own head and neck were in full view. I had a rifle with me and it did not take us many minutes to get to the fox and despatch him. It was a big fox; he weighed 23lb. 3oz. This is just about eight pounds over the average for this area and about eight pounds heavier than Bill.

I think Bill was a great character as dogs go. I hope you do too.

Bill Rose

His full name was William Rose, but I will refer to him as Bill.

Bill owned and farmed a small farm known as High Street Farm. This was situated about one mile from Old Weston on the road that leads to the Alconburys. It consisted of a farm house, a milking shed and numerous other buildings. There were some nineteen acres of land.

It is the late 1950s and early 1960s that I am writing about. Bill Rose was actually a cousin of my mother so of course I knew him fairly well and because his farm was on the edge of the Hamerton Estate I saw him on most days. Bill lived alone although he had a wife who visited him once in a while. They had a son and a daughter, both of whom were married. At that time Bill was not a recluse; he was just a man who never appeared to let anything worry him in any way at all. He never owned a car and if he wanted to go to town he would cycle to Old Weston either on a Saturday or a Wednesday and go by bus.

He was always tidy in his dress and on his farm but he just did not seem to care what day it was or what time it was. We would often share a bottle of beer and this was purchased through an off licence who delivered supplies once a fortnight. Bill paid one time and I paid the next time. He was very good company and when he was younger had indulged in a number of activities like poaching rabbits. He would often say to me, 'You know, Alb, no one ever ought to be prosecuted for poaching rabbits because it is the hardest money anybody could ever earn.' One day Bill said to me, 'If it is fine in the morning, come up and drive the old tractor for me. I will get the binder ready and we will cut that bit of spring wheat.' It was about three acres. It was fine on the following day and I was there to help get the job done but the tractor refused to start. Of course it was old and had to be started with a handle in the front end. Bill just laughed and said, 'Oh, she is often like that so we will go in the house and make a pot of tea. She will be all right when she has had a bit more time to think.' We had the tea and returned to the tractor which came to life at the first attempt. We cut the wheat.

On another afternoon I called in about half past two in the afternoon. The house door was open and the old dog lay in the kitchen. I said, 'Are you about, Bill?' There was not a reply so I walked across to the milking shed. Bill was milking one of his cows. I asked if he was going out.

He replied, 'No, Alb. What made you ask me that?'

I said, 'Well, Bill, I thought you were milking a bit early.'

He gave a little chuckle and said, 'No, Alb, I ain't early, you see, because this is the morning milking.

In the mid sixties Bill retired from farming and went to live with his daughter. He lived to a very good age and always seemed to be so cheerful and carefree.

Oscar Jordan

It was shortly after the last war that I first met Oscar. He was

Oscar Jordan.

married with a nice wife and three children, two sons and a daughter.

I was with a friend of mine, Len Fortescue. We had been out for the day following the Bucks Otterhounds in Bedfordshire and we called at Oscar's house on the way home. Oscar was a real hard working man and when we first met we realised that we had a lot in common. We both loved good working dogs especially terriers that went to ground to fox and badger. We were to spend many happy days and part days together. Oscar was with us at Holywell when Tubby Lupton drained the gin bottle: Oscar's comment at the time was, 'Bless his bloody guts.'

Oscar and I and numerous others spent a lot of time foxing with terriers. One day we were after fox on a farmer's land and the terriers were to ground in an old sand pit. The keeper who was employed by the farmer was named Sid and he said, 'There is something trying to push its way out of a small hole, just here.' My son Arthur said, 'Put your hand in, Sid, it won't bite.' Sid did just that and of course he was bitten and as he stood there with blood dripping off his hand, Oscar said, 'Sid, I thought you had more bloody sense than that.'

When the digging was deep and there was a lot of soil to be moved just give Oscar a big shovel and it was like a bulldozer at work.

In the 1960s Oscar decided that he would start bee keeping so I gave him several good hives and eventually these were stocked with bees. That was all right until Oscar decided to have a look inside the hives to see how the honey store was progressing. What actually occurred no one really seems to know but the bees were so antagonistic to him that they rendered him insensible. Later that day however I visited the site and put the hives back together and the bees were fairly passive. So my advice to novice beekeepers is to take advice from a person with experience before tackling the job alone.

Oscar progressed from an agricultural worker to being a game and pigeon dealer for Frostgame Ltd although in his own words it was bloody sticky going for a start. Then he bought a number of farm implements and also went into agricultural contracting and did very well but at all times he was ready to attend a day's shooting be it a hare shoot, a game shoot or just a day decoying pigeon. I believe that I gave him some of his most enjoyable days decoying pigeon.

During that period of time I owned and worked several good labradors and springer spaniels and so I received a number of invitations through Oscar to attend as a picker up at a variety of shoot days in his area. The days I enjoyed the most were at a Mr Spencer Thomas' Estate at Bushmead. I had met that gentleman over twenty years previously when he was a guest of my employer. Of course that had been when we had a lot of truly wild partridge. After I had spent the day at a shoot with Oscar we always had a meal together at Oscar's house; it was always a fine meal.

Oscar was at all times a fine and generous friend. There was another side to his character that not a lot of people knew about. He was always involved in organizing events to raise money for any worthy cause and when he was involved he certainly used all the energy and ingenuity that he possessed.

Oscar also loved a good singsong in a public house and his singing was to say the very least humorous and lively. One of his favourite renderings was that lovely hymn 'The Old Rugged Cross'. Of course he knew it all by heart.

But like a lot of good things, suddenly it all changed. In the summer of 1987 Oscar became ill. He just faded away and we lost him on 1 January 1988. He was sixty-one years of age. I often think about him; life was never dull when he was around.

Chippy Shadbolt

Chippy was in his eighties when I was in my thirties. Chippy was a native of Old Weston. I was a native of Winwick. Naturally I had known Chippy and his family for as long as I could remember. A tall lean man, he smoked and chewed twist tobacco I believe for the whole of his life. Like most agricultural workers of his time he was a good tradesman. He could and did work with horses; stack and thatch: trim, lay, stake and bind a hedge; dig a ditch or lay a drain. Also a keen gardener and allotment worker, as a spare time job he repaired cycles for all and sundry.

Now I will quote a little story told to me by my old friend Mervyn Joyce. It was around the 1930s. Mervyn, Chippy, and a number of other persons were acting as beaters on the Hamerton Estate on a shoot day. It was bitterly cold and at lunch time the beaters sheltered in a barn to have their lunch. At that time there were not any or at least very few thermos flasks so the food was cold. It had been taken to the barn by horse and cart. There were also several one-gallon jugs of beer. The day was so cold that very little of the beer was drunk. This worried Chippy; he said, 'If we don't drink it they won't send so much out another time,' and he helped solve the problem by consuming most of it himself. Of course when the time came to rise and shine after lunch Chippy could not get onto his feet and so had to be taken back to home base by horse and cart.

It was October 1948. Chippy had been digging potatoes on his allotment at the top end of Old Weston. The potatoes were not very large and as he wheeled them on the barrow down the street he was accosted by a farmer who had moved from the Fens to Old Weston just over a year earlier. The farmer looked at the potatoes and said, 'Pig potatoes, Chippy.' 'No,' replies Chippy. The farmer says, 'But they are too small for ware.' Chippy chews his cud of twist and spits at the farmer's feet and says, 'I have farmed that allotment for over fifty years; now you try growing potatoes on any one of your fields for forty years out of the next fifty and see how you get on.' He spits again and wheels his potatoes away.

Arthur Burrows

Arthur moved from Yaxley Fen to Old Weston in the summer of 1947. He bought a farm in that parish. A well built strong man, he was always at work. He farmed well and eventually bought two more farms, one at Brington and one at Hargrave. It seems that his only relaxation was to visit a public house on a Saturday evening, mostly the Wheatsheaf at Thurning. He would have a pint or two of beer and play skittles, a game that he enjoyed so much that win, lose, or draw he usually paid for the beer.

Arthur had a great sense of humour. He often told the story about the local man who asked him to sign his dole paper to say that he was available for work. Arthur told him, 'I can do better than that, I can find you a job.' The man replied, 'But I don't want your bloody job and if you ask me to drive a tractor I'll drive it into a

Arthur Burrows at work.

ditch and if you ask me to feed your bloody pigs, I'll let them all out.' Arthur said, 'So I signed his paper.'

One Saturday in January I helped organize a large hare shoot. We shot over almost all the land in the parishes of Old Weston and Winwick. Practically every farmer and land owner participated. The practice was to number all persons taking part and then to form two teams, the odd numbers being one team, the even numbers the other. One team did all the walking on the first drive and the second team did it on the next drive. So it was walk a drive and stand a drive throughout the whole day. On one drive I was walking next to Arthur. Arthur was using a very old twelve bore hammer shotgun. We walked along. A hare jumped up in front of Arthur. Up came the old gun. Arthur fired and hit the hare in the hind-quarters breaking both hind legs. Someone finished it off a few minutes later. Exactly the same thing was repeated, the same person finished the second hare off. He then said to Arthur, 'You are only hitting them in the arse,' and in a flash Arthur replied, 'Boy, when you are as old as my old gun you won't be able to get up to an old hare's arse.'

At the time that Arthur farmed at Old Weston I was employed as gamekeeper in that area. It was all partridge ground. Arthur kept his own sporting rights but we were allowed to drive over his land whenever we wished. One night in September long after nightfall I heard a shotgun being fired fairly regularly on Arthur's land so I rode over on my bike and observed what was going on. Someone was ploughing with a tractor and they were shooting at whatever they saw in the tractor's lights.

A couple of days later I saw Arthur and I said that someone was ploughing at night and shooting while doing so on his land. His reply was, 'Oh, that's all right, it was me.' As I turned to leave, he said, 'Would you do me a favour?'

I said, 'Yes, if it is within my power to do so.'

He said, 'In my garage are some partridges; would you take them and sell them for me because I do not have a game licence.'

When I entered his garage I found exactly ninety English partridge hung up.

On a great number of occasions Arthur said to me, "Ah boy, sixty is the dangerous age, if you get through sixty you go on to a good old age." One evening he collapsed and died in his own home. He was fifty-nine years of age.

Mrs Flo Daniels

This lady was aunt to my mother and so naturally was always referred to as Aunt Flo.

Aunt Flo and her husband Dave owned a small farm on the Fen not very far from Whittlesey. They never owned a tractor or a car but they owned a couple of horses to do the work on their land. A couple of cows provided them with milk and butter, poultry gave them eggs and a chicken to roast once in a while. They kept a few pigs so that they could have one slaughtered and this provided them with home cured bacon at all times. Dave could snare a hare or a rabbit or shoot a pheasant on their own land when these things were required. Oh, Dave knew how to do all these things very well; in fact, like a tremendous number of Fen people both Aunt Flo and Dave had a great knowledge of the ways of the wild.

I forgot to mention the trotting pony and the buggy. These two provided them with transport when they wished to go a little further afield. Of course I am writing about the period from 1945 to the 1950s.

Dave was a small wiry man with ginger hair and a ginger moustache. Aunt Flo was not very tall but very robust in build and of course they were both very strong as they needed to be to do all their own work on their land.

Aunt Flo had a beautiful face. It always looked as though it had been freshly washed and polished with cheeks like rosy apples and very blue twinkling eyes and she had such a happy temperament just as though life was one huge joke.

During the 1939–45 war, a portion of their land was taken over by the Air Ministry and their farm house was flattened to ground level. The Ministry erected a wooden building on the land that they had left as temporary accommodation. Aunt Flo and Dave soon had it all camouflaged with rambler roses. Aunt Flo would say, 'Yes, and we now have greenfly indoors as company for the cat and the mice.'

Now in the very early 1950s I drove down to visit Aunt Flo and Dave. My mother, my wife and two of our sons were with us. Of course they were tremendously pleased to see us but Arthur our second son who was nearly seven years of age refused to enter the dwelling. I asked him why and he said, 'It is like a hen roost, it isn't a house.' Of course, when I told Aunt Flo she laughed until the tears ran down her cheeks and then went out and, clucking like a hen, got him to come in.

When Aunt Flo and Dave were younger they had lost one of their two daughters when she was some fifteen years of age. It was some time before the war but from the day of her death the back door of Aunt Flo's house was never again closed, either by day or night. I once overheard her talking to my mother and she just made a simple statement. She said, 'May [that was my mother's name], we will never close the door because at some time our daughter may wish to visit us.' This was said without any emotion at all.

The hen roost lasted the two of them for the rest of their lives, although it was temporary accommodation.

J. L. Edwards

This is 1993 and if Jim Edwards lives until 11 August he will be eighty years of age. He has been a friend of mine for about sixty of those years.

Jim Edwards.

We have enjoyed some wonderful times together. Early in his married life he became a partner in his family's business which was road haulage. Then later in life he set up his own business, again haulage.

He was a tremendously hard working man but he was never too busy to find the time to go shooting or beating; it was his one great hobby. If it was spring or summertime every little bit of spare ground around his house would be occupied with coops and wire pens containing pheasant or partridge chicks and although there always seemed to be greater numbers than there should have been in the space where they were they always seemed to thrive. It was most surprising how well they always looked.

In the 1950s Jim looked after a shoot at Woolley. He did it all for nothing. It was his interest. However busy he was at his own or the family business he would always find time to visit his traps even if it meant visiting them after it was dark.

It was Jim who entirely by accident in 1963 caught a six-week-old badger cub in a Fenn trap that was at Woolley. Eric Goodwin and his wife Pearl reared and tamed the cub; they named it Bill. Bill was to gain great fame and notoriety locally for his antics and misdeeds but that is another story. Jim was also a practical joker: if a beater left his lunch bag unattended it was often found to contain a few pebbles instead of his lunch when lunch time came.

On one occasion Jim and a couple of others left the George at Spaldwick by the back door. It was after nightfall and Jim saw a small pick-up truck in the back yard, the property of a local man. Jim says to his two friends, 'Quick, boys, lift the back part up.' This was quickly done and Jim put bricks under the back axle so that when it was lowered the back wheels were clear of the ground. Later on the owner got in it to drive home and when he put it in gear it failed to move. The owner came to the conclusion that one of the half shafts must have broken so he walked home. Then next morning he phoned the local garage and instructed them to tow it to their garage and repair it. Of course the owner later was annoyed by people enquiring about the welfare of his half shaft. Fortunately it was a long time before it became known that Jim was the person responsible for that little joke.

On one occasion Jim, Tom, Joyce, Eric Goodwin and myself went on a four-day wildfowling trip. We did not get a lot of wildfowl but we had a very good time.

Jim always had a good dog in the shooting field. In the mid nineteen fifties he owned a yellow labrador named Kim. It had trained itself so was a bit unruly and a job to control but its scenting and working ability were absolutely terrific. If there was a bird that was dead or wounded but could not be found everyone would say, 'Send Jim with Kim; they will find it.' They usually did although one could never be certain because Jim usually had a dead bird in his game bag when he went in search of the lost bird.

Later on, after Kim became too old for work, Jim borrowed a trained springer spaniel bitch from me and this meant that when Jim borrowed it was for the whole of the bitch's life. Her name was Zipalong. Lively she was, of pedigree breeding and highly intelligent; she had a truly magnificent temperament and was one hundred per cent obedient. Without a doubt Zipalong was the best borrow Jim ever made. It was as Jim remarked on a number of occasions: whenever he and Zipalong went into a shooting field they knew that they would be invited to attend again. He said once Zip had been observed at work it was open sesame for the future. In my opinion that was Jim's happiest time. Zipalong was born in 1960; Jim borrowed her at the beginning of the 1961 season and of course it was for all of her life.

The next one was another springer spaniel bitch, Wayward Jill. This was a tremendously hard-working bitch though not so controllable as Zipalong had been but she served Jim very well at all times, giving him twelve good working years.

The next borrowing was again a springer spaniel bitch; her name was Princess Christina. Once again Jim was fortunate to borrow an

113

absolutely superb bitch, pretty to look at, absolutely obedient and top of her class in the shooting field. Oh, how she pleased Jim.

Christina was born in November 1974. Jim was still working Wayward Jill so he did not borrow Christina until 1978 and again he was to enjoy a number of wonderful seasons with her. Jim lost Christina in 1986. By this time of course Jim was like myself getting old but I owned a nice little six-year-old black labrador bitch named Fly Blow so Jim borrowed her. Fly Blow was in my opinion just right for Jim because Jim had slowed down tremendously and Fly Blow was of an easy steady temperament. They made a good very steady pair.

One might wonder why I always allowed Jim to borrow my dogs just as he wished? Well, he was my friend and it is possible that I am a bit stupid where my friends are concerned but I can remember one thing that made Jim special to me. In 1960 I had the opportunity to buy the property that I still live in and own. Now when Jim heard about my opportunity, he said, 'Now, you listen to me for once. You buy it. If you haven't got the money I will lend you whatever you need and you can have it tomorrow.' I have never forgotten.

Now we have got all the dog and the other business down in writing we must concentrate on Jim. Once more, he also had a lovely temperament. He never forgot a good turn or a bad turn and although he would never ever say much at any time he never forgot.

Jim was looking after a shoot for a syndicate in the late 1960s and his helpmate was Billy Wildman Senior. Billy's son, also Billy, is still alive and living at Ellington. Whenever it was possible I attended Jim's shoot days and Jim always attended mine. Jim was a good organizer; he would have made a first class gamekeeper, he was so interested, but at times when birds were rising thick and fast he would get so excited that it would be some little time before he realized that most of his companion beaters were standing watching what he was doing.

Sadly, Billy Wildman Senior died and for a while Jim was like a lost spirit. Then fortune smiled on him. Another retired gamekeeper had moved to Ellington; his name was Jack Legg. He was already known to Jim because Jack had been a beat keeper at Kimbolton so it was only natural that Jack became Jim's second in command and a good job he did as well. Jack was a very experienced man although unfortunately he did not enjoy the very best of health. I never ask him what was wrong with him. I suppose if I had I would have received the usual reply that gamekeepers give: 'Oh, I am all right except that I am crazy.'

Jim and Jack were to enjoy a number of happy years working together. Jim would often remark to me, 'You know exactly how it is, mate, it's a case of the old helping the old.'

In 1979 I was invited to spend a week on a grouse moor in Cumbria, not shooting, just helping out and when I asked the gentleman who invited me if I could take Jim along he replied at once, 'Of course, bring him along.' The gentleman had known Jim for a long time and so when the time came we duly arrived at Burnstones, close to Alston in Cumria. Jim had Princess Christina and I had her son with me; his name was Style.

Jim and I lived in what was known as the bothy. It was a wooden hut some twelve feet long and ten feet wide. It had a good roof and the walls were lined so it was warm and remember, it was the month of August but we were at about the eleven hundred foot altitude level. The bothy was furnished with two single beds, a couple of chairs, a wash basin etc., and we were very comfortable. In the morning all I had to do was get up, nip across the yard into the shooting lodge kitchen, a distance of about fifteen yards, boil a kettle of water, make a pot of tea, then back to the bothy where Jim and I could sit in bed and enjoy tea very well fortified with whisky. Once again, the life of Riley and who could wish for anything better?

Of course by nine o'clock in the morning we would be up on one of the various beats on the grouse moor. Perhaps I should explain about what I believe is a beat on a grouse moor. The whole of the moor at Burnstones consisted of some twenty-five thousand acres of ground. This was split up into five sections; each section was called a beat and on each of these sections or beats there was enough ground to give a full day shooting which meant that on that particular moor it was possible to hold five days shooting without going over the same section or beat twice. I do hope that explains the situation.

Of course I knew all the beats because I had been privileged to have been on that moor on a number of previous occasions. Oh, how Jim enjoyed that week and the friends we made. Jim was the type of person who had a natural ability to make a friend of almost anyone he talked with. He was always so kind and considerate that everyone loved him.

Jim was also over the moon with the way Princess Christina worked on grouse. It was as though she had been doing it for all her life.

I met a keeper on that moor. His Christian name was Len and he had spent all his working life on grouse moors. Now his dogs were exceptional. Len would often send his dogs half a mile across the moor after a drive in search of any grouse that had flown on after being hit. Once his dogs were out hunting he would not even watch them. I once asked him about this and he said in his thick Cumbrian accent, 'Whiir, mon, I dinna ken whut tha be abut but I ken tha'll find mi ifn tha finds a gruss.' Now translated I reckon this is what Len meant: Why, man, I don't know what they are doing but I know that they will find me if they find a grouse. I noticed that they always did. I wish I had had the time to have developed Len's friendship.

Of course our time on the moor came to an end and we had to return to our homes. To this day Jim declared that it was the most enjoyable holiday he ever had. I enjoyed it as well but there, I always enjoy being with Jim.

I could carry on writing about Jim for a long time but I will only write about one more thing. In the early 1980s Jim was no longer fit enough to be capable of doing a full day in the beating team so he would attend with his dog and do a bit of picking up. Even when he could no longer do that he would either turn up at the last shoot before Christmas at lunch time with a bottle of whisky to give the beaters a drink or he would instruct me to do so in his absence. I know this much: a person could search a long time for a truer friend and character than Jim Edwards.

Jim Yeoman

Jim Yeoman was a distant relative of Billy Yeoman who I wrote about earlier. They were both natives of Great Gidding. I must give you some idea of my comparatively brief knowledge of Jim by telling you that Jim Yeoman was a First World War veteran and I am a Second World War veteran. I well remember Jim at his mother's farmhouse, Upton Lodge, as far back as 1926. I was the ferret boy for Jim on his and his brother's pursuit of rabbits on every Sunday during the winter months. They were hectic times. Each rabbit we caught was worth sixpence but a farmworker's daily rate was five shillings per day. We caught a lot of rabbits and I did get a good dinner each Sunday before I cycled back home. It would consist of a slice of roast beef an inch thick, a large portion of Yorkshire pudding and all the potatoes I liked straight out of the iron pot. They still had their jackets on: manna from heaven to a hungry ferret boy.

The war came, the war went, I came home thirty years of age. Jim Yeoman was in his mid sixties. His health was not all that good. His main trouble was his lungs. He smoked and he worked in the harvest field on a combine harvester or in a grain store so he inhaled all that wonderful smoke and dust that is found in those places.

He was a physical wreck but he never lost his sense of humour or discarded his pipe. Jim loved a pint of beer and a game of nap. Nap is a card game usually played by four persons. If any person was playing nap with Jim and held his cards carelessly and Jim could see what cards he had Jim would say, 'Keep your cards up, mate, it spoils my fun if I know what you have in your hand.'

In 1959 Jim's mother had passed away and Jim was living in the Upton Lodge farmhouse by himself. I often called in to see him and on one occasion Jim said, 'Now I will make you laugh,' and this is what he told me. He had to take tablets to assist his breathing and the bottle containing the tablets stood on the kitchen shelf among a lot of other bottles. One day Jim found his bottle was empty and when he put his reading glasses on and looked on the label he said, 'For a full week I had three times a day been taking worm tablets for lambs.' He was highly amused.

Tom

During the first week of April 1992, my last aunt passed away. She was my Aunt Win and her home was at Totnes, Devon. Of course my youngest son, my daughter-in-law and I attended the funeral. Aunt Win was my favourite aunt.

The service was at Totnes Church and after the service we all drove to the cemetery for the burial. Leaning on the stone wall at the entrance was a stocky overweight gentleman. He was elderly with very high colour in his face and smoking a cigarette. He walked down to the graveside very slowly with help of a walking stick. My cousin Ann introduced me to this gentleman. 'Albert, this is Tom, Tom, this is Albert.' Straight away Tom said, 'It is uphill to the church so I didn't get there but Win would not mind; she knows that I can't walk uphill and I need a stick to walk downhill.' Then after a couple of puffs on his cigarette and a cough or two, he says, 'Of course, Albert, I feel that I have known you for years. You see, your Uncle Richard and Win told me all about you.' It transpired that Tom owned a farm and was a great friend of my Uncle Richard and my Aunt Win who for years had owned a shop at 44 Fore Street, Totnes. They sold guns, cartridges, cycles, wirelesses and televisions.

We eventually got sat down in my aunt's house. Tom and I had two chairs side by side and a small table before us. Tom told me all about his farm and the shooting. Eventually tea and sandwiches were placed on the table, also a bottle of whisky. Tom drank some of his tea and topped it up with whisky. He took a drink and a couple of puffs at his cigarette and this is what he said. 'You know, Albert, if I had taken any notice of my doctor I would have died years ago.' He took another drink and a couple of puffs. 'He told me that if I didn't stop smoking and drinking whisky I would not live very long,' another drink, a couple of puffs, 'Of course he told me that twenty-five years ago. Of course he never drank or smoked himself but he died ten years ago.' Tom took a long drink and several puffs, and sat back in his chair, a cup in one hand, a cigarette in the other, a smile on his face, Oh, how I wished I had my camera with me, I could have had a photograph of a happy man at a funeral.

At the end of writing about Tom at my Aunt Win's funeral at Totnes I was of a good mind to call it a day saying enough is enough. Then casting my mind back I realised there were a tremendous number of what I call interesting people and incidents that I had failed to mention so after a break of almost a year I will attempt to pick it up once more.

Pickle

Pickle was a terrier, a remarkable terrier, born on 30 September 1962. She died in June 1976. Please understand that all my life I have admired and loved good working terriers and without a doubt have owned and worked some of the very best.

Also without a doubt Pickle was in my opinion one of the best. Her dam was a bitch of my own breeding named Lively. She was a great terrier with but one fault: she would never come out of an

The local policeman, Grove Wood 1976.

earth or drain as long as there was a fox or a badger in front of her. On one occasion Lively stayed to ground for seven days and seven nights and on another occasion for twenty-six hours. On both these occasions she had to be dug out with a mechanical digger. Lively died at the age of eighteen years and three months.

The sire of Pickle was that great terrier named Rusty. He was owned by Arthur Corby who lived at Wymington in the Oakley Hunt country.

Pickle was the smallest whelp in the litter. Like her dam she was white with tan markings. Being the smallest she received more fuss and care than her brothers and sisters so by six weeks of age she got to live in the house as one of the family and this was where she remained for the rest of her life when not out working with me in the countryside.

As a puppy she developed a great love for a bar of chocolate and a cup of tea, coffee or chocolate. These luxuries became a life-long habit with her.

Although being very small, her weight never exceeding eight and a half pounds, she was very agile and quickly showed her independence. At all times her nature towards other dogs and humans was kind and never in the whole of her life was she known to fall out or even growl at another dog above or below ground.

Her entry to work underground was by following her mother and grandmother and by the time she was two years old it was always Pickle who led the rest above and below ground.

This bitch never in her whole life bayed at a rabbit although she did a lot of work when we were rabbit catching.

Absolutely fearless, the biggest earth or the longest drain held no terrors for her. On numerous occasions she bolted foxes from drains five or six hundred yards long and on one occasion when she was six years of age we dug an old vixen out of an earth that Pickle had eventually got into a dead end and when I picked the little bitch up her left eyeball was hanging out of its socket. This meant an operation by the local vet who made a successful job of replacing the eye but she sadly lost part of her sight.

During the same year I dug out a dog fox she had worked into a dead end and when I picked her up and examined her the fox had removed most of her front teeth. But like the previous occasion when her eye was bitten out, never a whine or a whimper was heard from her and she just kept on working.

On three separate occasions this bitch bolted foxes from drains that had only one entrance. How she managed to get past the fox in a nine-inch pipe and then bolt it from the end she herself had entered no one will ever know, but she did it without getting badly bitten at any time.

Absolutely certain and true, when a fox was at home Pickle bore no malice towards other creatures except the badger. She would hunt and sometimes catch a rabbit but would never interfere with poultry, sheep or even young game birds. I could take her with me when feeding young game birds and she would just lie on her belly and watch them. If she had gone to ground in an occupied fox earth I had only to shout down the hole, 'Pickle, come out. We're going home!' and sure enough out she would come with of course many a backward glance at the earth.

She knew everyone who had been out with us after foxes and always made a great fuss of them if anyone said the word 'fox'. Even when in the house she would trot to the door and give a litttle yap and wag her tail as much as if to say, 'Well, here I am, all ready to go!'

We did try breeding with her on just one occasion but she was so small that although we did manage to get five pups from her only one of them survived. We named him Coffee and gave him to Frank Hufford who lived at Barham. Coffee was a grand terrier and served Frank well for many years.

I could write a book about Pickle but all that I will say is that I feel tremendously privileged to have owned and had the pleasure of working with such an honest and intelligent little bitch. But perhaps I should put it another way and say I was privileged to have been owned by such a bitch, for I am sure that was how she felt about it.

There are two more incidents that I feel I must write about. It had been obvious for some time that Pickle was failing and in mid-April 1976 she suffered a severe heart attack and was in a coma for about an hour. For a week after this she was very very unsteady but after that she appeared to make a good recovery. A couple of weeks later she became listless and often refused to eat. Of course, I still took her with me whenever I went after foxes and she worked as well and happily as ever she had done in her earlier days. In fact we got two foxes out of an earth only six days before she died, and how she showed her gratitude. Some people will say it was cruel to work a sick dog but Pickle always sensed when something was going on and all her life she had never been left behind so I believe it would have been much more cruel to have left her shut up at home and broken her brave little heart.

There is just one more incident in the story of Pickle. She had one very special friend, another terrier bitch called Pippa. Pippa was not closely related to Pickle but they were very much alike and there was only six weeks difference in their ages. Pickle was white with tan markings on her head and back while Pippa was white with black markings. She was a little heavier and more robust than Pickle.

Pippa was a very good bitch to work above or below ground but she just did not have the character of Pickle. If Pickle had been out and had a successful day, as soon as we were home she would strut around our living room with her tail upright and her head held high as if to say, 'Look at me. I am the best in the whole world!' Pickle and Pippa were inseparable. It was our practice to open the house door last thing at night and let them out onto the lawn for a run. They would go out together, have a run round and come back in together.

The day after Pickle died I buried her in my back garden and from that moment Pippa refused all food and drink. I buried her just ten days later. She had died of a broken heart. It was some time before our family recovered from that double tragedy.

Bill Brady

Bill was a corporal in our regimental police in the 10th Battalion the Parachute Regiment. After we returned from Holland in 1944 we lived in a camp at Ashwell which is about a mile and a half from Oakham which, at that time, was in the county of Rutland.

As a boy Bill had lived in London's East End. He had joined the Army as a boy soldier in 1934 or '35 so he was a fairly rugged sort of person as indeed he needed to be to maintain law and order in a parachute regiment. Anyhow, at the time we were at Ashwell members of our unit were allowed to visit Leicester on so many evenings each week. One Saturday night Bill was on patrol with two of his camp police in a jeep to keep order in the town. All of the liberty lorries had left town for camp at Ashwell and Bill realised that there were a fair number of our unit still in town. It was about twenty-four miles from Leicester to Ashwell so he told one of his men to get as many of them together as possible. Then he watched at the town's public toilets and eventually a bus driven by a lady driver stopped outside the toilets and the driver nipped into the toilet just as smartly as Bill nipped into the bus. Luckily the keys were still in the ignition so he was away to pick up the lads and drove them back to camp. Next morning Bill rang up the bus company and reported a bus without a driver on the roadside outside the camp. The local police came enquiring, of course, but it was a waste of time. A driver was brought from Leicester and as far as I know that was the end of the incident. Liberty lorries were used to transport men to and from Leicester, usually leaving town about 2330 hours.

On another occasion Bill Brady was on patrol in Oakham in his capacity of corporal of our regimental police responsible for the behaviour of our unit. Again he had two of his men with a jeep with him. During the evening he became involved in a card game in one of the hostelries that went on long after closing time. Bill had instructed his two men to return to camp by midnight if all was quiet in the town and when he was ready he would walk back to barracks, about one and a half miles away.

When the card game was over as well as the beer drinking, Bill set off on foot for camp. It was a moonlit night and as he walked along Ashwell Road he spotted a gent's cycle standing in a covered passageway between two houses so he wheeled it out into the road and cycled back to camp. Please bear in mind there were no street lights and all the houses were blacked out.

Next morning in the light of day and with a beer-free brain he saw that the cycle was a good quality machine. It was a Rudge Whitworth All-weather model with a three-speed and oilbath chain cover enamelled green. Once again Bill's brain came to his aid. A little later in the morning he got the police jeep, carefully loaded the cycle and drove to the police station in Oakham and wheeled in the cycle. He told the officer behind the desk that during his camp rounds that morning he observed the cycle leaning against one of the barrack blocks. He'd made enquiries but everyone denied all knowledge of it so he came to the conclusion that someone in the unit had borrowed it. The officer wrote down Bill's name, rank and number and gave Bill a receipt for the cycle.

Several days later a constable came into camp and was directed to Bill's office. He asked Bill if he would call at the police station sometime during the next forty-eight hours.

Bill went into town and the officer behind the desk at the police station told him that the owner of the cycle had proved it was his and claimed it. He was so pleased it had been recovered undamaged that he had left a reward of £2 for Bill. He signed the chitty for the reward and assured the officer that if by any chance he ever found out who had taken the cycle he would see the offender was punished. All said without even a glimmer of a smile on Bill's face.

The reader may think we had some rum sort of men in our unit. Well, of course we did, but so did all the other units in wartime. To give you an idea of what I mean, while I was in Egypt and a member of a Commando Unit a corporal was six hours late after a thirty-six hour pass he had spent in Ismailia. Of course, he made the excuse when brought up before the commanding officer that he had walked back to camp, a distance of some twenty kilometres. At this the colonel exploded and said, 'After all the training on using your own initiative you have been given you give me an excuse like that. If you had returned to camp riding on a donkey I would have let you off but you are not suitable to lead your section so you are reduced to the ranks,' – and he was.

In January 1945 our battalion was absorbed as reinforcements for the 2nd Parachute Battalion and I lost contact with Bill Brady so I cannot complete the story but I am pretty certain that if I had known it all it would have been very interesting.

Eric Abblitt

It was in 1961 that I first had the pleasure of meeting and talking with Eric. He had just purchased Grange Farm in the parish of Steeple Gidding. It was not a large farm, almost a square of agricultural land with the buildings and farmhouse almost at its centre.

Right along its northern boundary was a bridle way which I and a number of other people often walked along to get to Aversley Wood. A couple of my friends who lived in Sawtry at that time were responsible for the control of predators in Aversley Wood in the interest of conserving wild game. Aversley Wood belonged to Major Fitton who lived at White Hall, Sawtry. The two part-time keepers were Tom Joyce and Malcolm Houghton, both of whom had a good knowledge of the ways of the wild.

On a Sunday morning several of my friends and I were making

Eric Abblitt.

our way along the bridleway accompanied by a number of my terriers. We also carried several shotguns and spades. We met a man who was very interested in where we were going and what we intended to do so of course we explained that we hoped to locate and deal with a predator or, better still, several predators, in Aversley Wood. This gentleman at once showed great interest and he told us his name was Eric Abblitt and that he was the new owner of Grange Farm. We then introduced ourselves. Eric was in his mid-fifties, of medium height but very wiry, not a spare ounce of fat on him. His rugged features and weathered skin told us he'd spent much of his time in the open air. We later discovered he was a Fenman, and there is no hardier breed in the United Kingdom. At that time not one of us realised that we had met a man who was to become a good and true friend for a great number of years.

The outcome of that day was that Eric joined us on our expedition which was very successful and he was to become a regular member of our predator control group. He was a very valuable person to

A shoot day in Aversley Wood.

have as a friend; it didn't matter it if was work or play, Eric was always game to have a go. If we were hunting predators, shooting pigeons or any type of game we called that play, but when it came to clearing overgrown rides and pathways in Aversley Wood which we did annually for a number of years, that was classed as work. Because we did it all on a voluntary basis for no pay at all we worked a darned sight harder than any employer would have expected his hired men to.

As time went on a number of local landowners got to know Eric and so he became a regular guest at game shoots in the area and I am certain that the more he mixed with local people the more he became respected and popular, but Eric was not a person to be taken for granted by all and sundry, oh no. When the occasion arose he could be absolutely a John Blunt and very straight spoken.

Of course, as I was gamekeeper at Hamerton Eric was once in a while a guest there but more often he was with us when we carried out organised hare shoots. On these occasions we usually had the support of a number of the local farmers who enjoyed an opportunity to invite a friend or two to take part. In a well organised hare shoot the total bag at that time would be in excess of three hundred hares as well as a few rabbits and pigeon. Eric enjoyed those days very much.

Now there are no more hare shoots for the simple reason that the poachers with their running dogs have killed the local population to the point of near extermination.

Now back to Eric. I was, and still am, privileged to be classed as his friend and he is as indestructible as ever. In October 1991, along with his two grandsons, he accompanied me on an evening's duck flight and it says a lot for his eyesight that he accounted for several duck in the failing light. It was the seventeenth of the month and Eric's ninetieth birthday.

We will go back a few years to the 1980s. A group of us, including Eric, had obtained the sporting rights of Aversley Wood. Eric did all the business side of it and a very good job he had made

Aversley Wood.

of it too. We always knew exactly how the cash position was and we enjoyed some very good days' sport. Eric was always there with his dogs and his gun and we found that he was an exceptionally good shot.

In the days before Eric's two sons switched mainly to cereal farming we enjoyed at least one good shooting day on their land and of course the hospitality was of the highest order. What do I mean by cereal farming? In Eric's day he always grew a field or two of sugar beet and potatoes. These crops helped the wild pheasants because they provided both food and cover but when it became more lucrative to grow just corn the land was near naked, ploughed throughout the winter months with no food or shelter for the wild game.

Eric is now in his nineties and still very active. He makes a very effective job of his garden and his mind has lost none of its sharpness. It had to be an exceedingly rough day for Eric to be found indoors. He has a small garage cum workshop where he loves to tinker about. He may be fashioning a walking stick or perhaps working on a piece of machinery. He always keeps his workshop well organised and he knows exactly where to find every tool, bolt, screw or nail.

He is a good friend and jolly good company and I hope he lasts a long time yet.

I dare not write about Ev who is Eric's wonderful wife as she would probably scold me and beat me up so I will just say she is wonderful – all seven stone of her.

Bernard Nethercote Bletsoe

It was in the late 1940s that Bernard Bletsoe and his wife, Phyllis May, came to live and work at Grove Farm, Great Gidding. Until then I was not aware of his existence.

Bernard was a tall man, wiry and muscular, and it soon became apparent that he was a very keen supporter of all types of blood sports, especially riding to hounds in pursuit of the fox. He was a very fine horseman and a fine judge of horseflesh and he owned a splendid mare named Selmis. He rode her himself at the local hunt point-to-point meetings; the local pack were, and still are, the Fitzwilliam Foxhounds. In fact, Grove Farm where he lived and worked was owned by the Fitzwilliam family and was part of the Milton Estates.

Bernard Bletsoe riding Selmis won many races at point-to-point meetings, including the Fitzwilliam, the Cottesmore, the Fernie, the Quorn, the Oakley, the Woodland and Pytchley and the Pytchley. These were two separate packs, the Woodland and Pytchley being kennelled at Brigstock, the Pytchley at Brixworth, both in the county of Northamptonshire.

Perhaps I should explain what is meant by a point-to-point race meeting. At the end of each hunting season it is the practice for each pack of hounds to hold a horse race meeting to entertain their supporters and the landowners and farmers over whose land they hunted during the winter. They would be honoured guests with free passes and as much time was spent in the refreshment tent as watching the races so a good time was had by all. The public also enjoyed their day in the countryside though they often came away poorer rather than richer as the horses had little form to make betting a certainty.

The racecourse was usually roughly circular and some four and a half miles overall. There were always a good number of fences to be negotiated varying from a neatly trimmed quickthorn to post-and-rails and at some cases a water jump as well.

The race card might read like this. Race 1: Members only – men's race. Race 2: Members only – ladies' race. Race 3: Adjacent Hunts men's race. Race 4: Adjacent Hunts ladies' race. Then there could be races for heavyweight riders. Whatever happened it was always a very interesting day out. They are usually run under National Hunt Rules and the grandest of all is the annual Grand National.

Back to Bernard Bletsoe. He was often to be found attending a meet of the Bucks Otterhounds which were kennelled at Linslade. They were owned by the Uthwatts and the huntsman in my time was Lionel Dowse. The otterhounds hunted the Ouse, Nene and Welland valleys until the scarcity of otters made it impossible to carry on so it was discontinued in the early 1970s.

The reason for otter scarcity was water pollution, mainly through detergents. As the human race got cleaner so the water got dirtier. Now we are doing the same with the air we breathe.

A friend of mine, Walter Scott, carried out the research on the loss of the otters in the districts mentioned and he gave me a copy of his report.

There is one other person I must mention. His name was Doggy Robinson. He had been huntsman with the Bucks Otterhounds for many years and still followed hounds but it soon became obvious that his greatest interest was in testing the quality of the spirits in the various public houses in the area being hunted and he appeared to enjoy it.

In the early 1950s Bernard Bletsoe became interested in wildfowl of all species so he had a pond excavated and fenced in and built up a good collection during the first nesting season. He had trouble with carrion crows stealing the eggs so he waited with his gun for them to arrive. He shot at the first crow but only broke its wing. After he had caught it he felt sorry for it so he put it in a box for a cage, made splints for its wing and looked after it. When the wing was healed he released it back into the wild.

Bernard had a number of fox earths on the farm and if hounds ran a fox to ground in one of them he would ask how far he had been hunted. If the fox had given the hounds a good run he would say, 'Don't bolt him. He may give you a good run on another day.' But if the fox had gone to ground after only being hunted for a short time then he would say, 'Bolt him. A bit more exercise will do him good.'

After otter hunting ceased various packs of hounds were got together to hunt mink and in the spring of 1979 Bernard invited a pack to meet at Grove Farm. I had been invited and while the sherry and sandwiches were being handed round he asked me if I was being looked after and what I thought of the gathering. I said I thought they looked OK. He said with a twinkle in his eye, 'Yes, they are, but I think it's a gathering of rogues and ratcatchers.'

Bernard was the last of the farmers in this area to carry on with the old farming methods known as mixed farming. He did not remove hedgerows and he did not believe in the burning of stubble fields. He kept a mixture of stock including cows for rearing calves, bullocks for fattening, a flock of sheep, a good number of pigs and free-range poultry, a number of which were often killed by the foxes on his own land. He considered it to be a natural event and made no trouble about it although I thought it was a little bit like a banker keeping his own bank robbers. Bernard, by carrying on with his mixed farming, used all his straw and hay on his own farm for litter and feed for his own stock and, of course, it was returned to the land in the form of manure which without a doubt was very good husbandry.

He was the last farmer in the area to make good use of workhorses and horse-drawn carts and wagons. The one disadvantage to this system is that livestock need regular attention on every day of the year.

Now here's a little story that was told to me today, 27 January 1994, by the wife of Richard Warrener who lives and farms at Holly Lodge in the parish of Buckworth and who was bequeathed all his flamingos by the late Bernard Bletsoe. The flamingos are still alive.

This is what the lady told me. Several years before his death a flamingo escaped from Bernard's wildfowl compound and Bernard even hired a helicopter to fly over the area in search of it. Then one day he stopped and asked some council workmen if by any chance they had seen a flamingo on their travels and he was highly amused when one of the men replied, 'No, mister, and we ain't seen no barrage balloon neither.' Of course the workmen were not local so they didn't know Bernard.

There was one tremendously sad event in the lives of Bernard and his wife. For several years a young man lived in the house with them. He was employed as a groom and was a very likeable young man. In November 1963 he was electrocuted while preparing to clip a horse with a set of faulty clippers. This was very upsetting but as always after it happens it was too late. The lad's name was William Larratt.

There is one thing of which I am very sure and that is that the death of Bernard N. Bletsoe on 26 May 1989 was a sad loss to the land. He was seventy-one years old, a true man of the land who had placed good husbandry before financial gain.

Stan Robbins

It was shortly after the end of the Second World War that I first met Stan Robbins. He, like myself, loved working terriers so of course that is what first brought us together. A number of us were going out after foxes with terriers and Oscar Jordan, who was one of my best friends, brought Stan along; they both lived at Little Staughton.

Nearly all of the Beating Team. Stan Robbins giving Bell's Whisky a free advert.
Left to Right: C. Slack; P. Hall; M. Alderman; myself; V. Dawkes; S. Robbins; T. Masters; S. Templar.

Groveswood, 1995. Left to right: Mark Smith; Arthur Spring.

Stan was, and still is, a big man over six feet tall and weighing in the region of fourteen stone without being fat. He is a very bright, cheerful person with a good sense of humour, illustrated thus. One day in the shooting field he observed a fellow beater filling his lunch bag with apples from an orchard. When he left it unattended Stan removed the apples and replaced them with the equivalent weight in stones. It is strange but the victim of that joke never, as far as I know, mentioned the incident.

Stan and I were to spend a lot of time together as beaters in the shooting field and catching rabbits with ferrets. We also went after the odd fox with our terriers but this didn't happen very often until he came to live in Alconbury Weston when he retired and between us we still own several useful terriers.

136

Now that I am getting a bit long in the tooth Stan has to do most of the digging and weight carrying while I trace the ferrets when they are underground with a small pocket-size radio locator. We have some fun together but there is not the number of rabbits in our area that there used to be and we can see even our bit of fun with the ferrets coming to an end very soon but at least we have enjoyed ourselves while we could. Stan is always very good company and a good friend; he is a man for all places at all times.

End of Story

A couple of years ago one of my sons said, 'Why don't you write about the people you seem to like to talk about,' so after giving it some thought that is exactly what I have done.

In the whole of the writing I have kept to the truth of the events and the correct names of people and places.

All this has been done from memory, of course, and special dates like a death are, as far as I could check, correct. The commencement of the writing is roughly from about 1921 which is as far back as I can distinctly remember.

Naturally I have only written about people who I thought were, shall we say, a little bit out of the ordinary either in the things they said and did or in the tales they told.

One little item that I failed to write about George Hull. It was a sunny summer's afternoon in about 1927. George sat on his front doorstep enjoying the sunshine and smoking his pipe. His nine-year-old grandson, also George, was bouncing a tennis ball on the window panes when old George said, 'You can stop that before you break the window.' The lad took no notice and carried on. 'Stop that,' said George, 'and I won't tell you again.' The grandson still carried on. Without a word George stood up, broke every pane in the window with his bare fist and sat down again. 'That will save you breaking them,' he said. I witnessed this first-hand as I

Stan Robbins.

was sitting on the grass not ten yards away talking with George's other grandson, Tommy.

Yes, George was a real character.

That's all.